DATE DUE			
~~Oct11'74~~			
Dec3 80			

THE WAR DISEASE

by the same author

THE BRIDGE OF REASON

THE EMPEROR'S NEW CLOTHES

the war disease

by Norman Z. Alcock

Cover design: Susan M. Allison

CPRI Press. Oakville. Ontario.

Published by CPRI Press
CPRI Press is operated by the
Canadian Peace Research Institute, Oakville, Ontario

To the prophets and scholars
whose early widom laid the groundwork
for our present understanding of war

acknowledgments

The points of view expressed in this study are my own. But this book could never have been written or published were it not for rigorous editorial assistance by John Millyard, Ralph Buchsbaum (of Boxwood Press) and Peter Wright (of Penguin Books); careful attention to publication details by Rosemary Maxfield, Virginia Young, Merv Davidson, Jim Wert and Mary Robitaille; trenchant comments by other colleagues at the Canadian Peace Research Institute, Hanna and Alan Newcombe, Bill Eckhardt, and some distant colleagues, Ted Lentz, Jerome Laulicht, J. D. Dash, Anatol Rapoport, Paul Smoker, Ellis Fullerton, Betty and Walter Morgan, all of whom read and criticized an earlier draft. I should like to acknowledge and thank each of them.

My wife Patricia assisted in every way and as well offered that constant encouragement so necessary to any author.

The Canada Council, Leitch Transport and supporters of the Canadian Peace Research Institute provided financial assistance over the years for much of this project.

foreword

In a small booklet (Alcock, 1961) published in 1961, I had the temerity to say that "in the five or ten years left to us they (the peace researchers) may be our brightest hope."

The ten years have elapsed. In that time a half-dozen research centres have swelled to more than three dozen; two international peace research associations with members from East and West have been formed; six new international peace research journals have been added to the single journal being published in 1961; two agencies of the United Nations—UNESCO and UNITAR—have become involved; several national governments have recognized the importance of peace research and set up institutes; agencies or committees.

But it is unlikely, in spite of these encouraging signs, that a great rush of scientific talent will invade this new field, for peace research must be supported, and its support comes from a special kind of person. He must be well-educated, reasonably uncommitted ideologically, and have a high sense of social responsibility. (Laulicht and Alcock, 1966.) Such people are rare.

Nevertheless, I must confess to a sort of desperate optimism, for in the past 11 years enough substantial research has been published to begin to define with precision the causes of war. This book is an interim attempt to formulate that definition. It is addressed to two groups: the concerned public (potential supporters of peace research) and the scientific community (potential peace researchers). The book assumes throughout that a logical analysis of the causes of war can be made from the available evidence. Where I am familiar with the research I have quoted from the primary source, but where the research is in an unfamiliar discipline I have sometimes used a secondary source.

In such a short book, it is obvious that some good and important studies have been omitted; my apologies to the scholars neglected. I believe, however, that the studies which are included are representative of the essential streams of contemporary science.

Characteristically, a scientist will not burst into print with a set of tentative conclusions. In defence of violating this cardinal ethic, I can only say man still is running a perilous race where global catastrophe is no more than a telephone call or push-button away.

Two essential problems face us as scientists, politicians, or concerned individuals: first, the research data obtained to date and the analysis resulting from them must be confirmed; second, if the analysis of this study is correct, we still must learn how to act properly and effectively on these results.

Finally, though the results of my analysis are encouraging, a great deal of research remains to be done. Whether the time left for doing it is five years—or even twenty-five years—the stakes seem worth a bigger effort than is being made today, for the stakes are the fate of mankind.

Norman Alcock
Canadian Peace Research Institute
Oakville, Ontario, Canada
March 1972.

contents

1 introduction

Throughout the ages man has gazed at the stars and pondered the secret of their motion. As early as the 4th century B.C. Aristotle thought he had the answer when he wrote: "A moving body comes to a standstill when the force which pushes it no longer acts." But not until the 17th century were the rhythms of the heavenly bodies finally understood, when careful observations by Galileo and precise calculations by Newton established that: "A moving body persists in its state of motion, unless compelled to change by an external force." Why was the difference between the two views so important? Because only when Aristotle's false conclusion was thoroughly disproved could the science of physics progress. It has been said that Aristotle's great authority throughout Europe held back our understanding of the nature of the physical world for more than one thousand years (Einstein and Infeld, 1938).

Throughout the ages man has yearned for peace, and wondered at his own warlike nature.

Put up thy sword into his place, for all they

> that take the sword shall perish with the sword.
>
> I say unto you 'love your enemies, do good to them which hate you.'
>
> ... unto him that smiteth thee on the cheek offer also the other.

Thus said Jesus of Nazareth 19 centuries ago.

Can it be that Christ's teachings are just as misleading to our understanding of war as were Aristotle's teachings to our understanding of physics? Perhaps, however, the teachings are right, or perhaps they are partial truths. This book is an attempt to find answers to these queries, for it is a brief account of the findings of peace research. Such findings should be of interest to that third of the world which calls itself Christian, for though Jesus did not directly apply his sermons to the problem of war, his followers often do.

Peace research is an inter-disciplinary scientific search for the causes of war and for cures and preventions which may help to eliminate this ancient scourge. The scientific investigation of war has not yet found its Galileo or Newton for no single startling discovery has given the lead to much subsequent research. But early predecessors there are: the American political scientist Quincy Wright; the English mathematician Lewis Richardson; the Austrian ethologist Konrad Lorenz; and the physician of the mind, Sigmund Freud. They have all shown that there could be a science of peace, that the social illness of war follows understandable patterns, and is capable of systematic investigation.

A second third of the world's population calls itself socialist and subscribes to the teachings of Karl Marx. There is reason to suppose the words of Marx, like those of Christ, may be in error in pinpointing the causes of war and the means to its final abolition. To find out, once again we can turn to the results of research and the strength of the case will depend on the quality of the evidence.

Since two-thirds of the world's population is steeped in either Christian or Marxist thought, it is important to question and where possible to verify any of their lessons which apply directly to war. Aristotle, we will recall, had a profound influence on modern thought, but we have discovered on the basis of scientific evidence not to revere all of his thoughts equally. Let us follow the same course with the prophets.

Can science really solve such an intractable problem as war, or even move mankind closer to peace? The world is a healthier place to live in than it was a century ago, and I believe a parallel can be drawn between our efforts to eliminate disease and our efforts to eliminate war. In 1864 Louis Pasteur suggested, following observations and experiments, that invisible organisms called germs, which were always present in ordinary air, caused putrefaction. Based on Pasteur's conclusions, Joseph Lister in 1865 predicted that, if putrefaction were caused neither by spontaneous generation of germs nor by oxygen in the air (earlier theories) but by germs already in the air, then surgery would be enormously helped if a chemical could be found to keep these germs away from patients. The dramatic proof of his case—the effective use two years later of carbolic acid—helped confirm Pasteur's theory. Pasteur's theory was not complete. It did not explain all illness—virus infection, genetic errors, and psychosomatic disorders, for example—because disease is not a simple matter with a single cause. But Pasteur's theory, incomplete as it was, did move medicine forward and made an incalculable contribution to every man's well being. Similarly, we may hope that as peace research adds to our knowledge—though not necessarily our complete understanding—of the causes of war, we will be in a better position to build a stable peace. This book is based on that assumption.

Can success in treating diseases of the individual be cited as hope for similar successes in treating the social affliction of war? Some of the greatest minds in medical history believed so. As Dr. Alexander Haddow once said: "... there can be little doubt either of the need, the urgent need, for the work of our Association (the Medical Association for the Prevention of War), or of our debt to its founders. If any doubt remains, let us remember the tradition of Pasteur, Virchow, Pavlov, and Schweitzer—who all believed there was a science not only of illness, but also of crime and war." (Haddow, 1963.)

We have traveled a long way down the path towards a warless world, and though the end of that path still lies ahead of us, it is at least within sight. It is that close because peace researchers, like medical researchers, are equipped with the scientific method.

In documenting this investigation of the disease of

war most of this book will contain facts discovered through biological and sociological research. The research results then will be synthesized into a theory that explains war. The answer is not perfect, but it is the best we can formulate to date. If nothing else, this analysis will serve as a guidepost or a springboard to much more work which, hopefully, will lead to the prevention of one of man's most frightful problems: his own extinction.

But before we go on to catalog recent research, let us look at some of the better known conventional theories of the causes of war.

2 conventional theories

THE ARMS RACE

The "arms race" theory is based on the idea that wars often result from a process of action and reaction between two nations or two groups of nations. The existence of armaments in nation A threatens the security of nation B, which then feels compelled to increase its military appropriations, in turn causing nation A to "escalate" still further. The result can be a leveling off, due in part to the financial burden of the defence expenditures. More often, the arms race can explode into war.

Philip Noel-Baker, distinguished disarmament expert and winner of the Nobel Peace prize for The Arms Race, presents impressive historical evidence that the very existence of armaments was a significant factor in precipitating World Wars I and II. He linked arms production not only to fear of an enemy nation and the need for security, but also to the profit motive of the arms industry. "The arms race was not the sole cause of war, but it was a powerful and contributory cause ... it influenced governments both in their general policy, and at moments of crisis," Noel-Baker wrote. "Above all, it kept alive the anachronistic idea that wars are inevitable." (Noel-Baker, 1958, p. 74.)

C. Wright Mills, in The Causes of World War III, indicts a number of groups for their responsibility in the world-wide drift towards a nuclear holocaust: the scientists engaged in military development, the religious institutions which have become a "willing spiritual means and a psychiatric aide of the nation-state" (Mills, 1958, p. 74) and the nation-state itself. But he too, concludes that the "immediate cause of World War III is the preparation of it." (Mills, 1958, p. 149).

If the weapons system itself and its evil corollary, the arms race, is the principal cause of war, then an obvious solution is disarmament. An ancient notion, and a Christian one, but one which seldom has been wholeheartedly tried. Perhaps with good reason. In 1955, for instance, after Costa Rica had unilaterally disarmed, she was invaded by her neighbour Nicaragua. Costa Rica quickly redressed the balance by purchasing four modern fighter planes.

A more practical approach, perhaps, is not unilateral but bilateral disarmament. If an arms race can escalate, why can it not under suitable inducements—such as mutual fear—be made to deescalate? Such an alternative has been proposed in some detail by psychologist Charles Osgood. He pictures two men on a teeter-totter; both carefully move towards (rather than away from) the center, with plenty of warning from both sides before either makes a move (Osgood, 1962.) Disarmament also can be negotiated, not "unnegotiated" as Osgood suggests. Indeed, negotiated bilateral disarmament is the type of disarmament which is generally considered by statesmen today and which makes the news—especially when there has been a failure to reach agreement.

Is disarmament the way to end war? Yes, if really possible, but there is evidence to be presented later, which indicates that it is not a reliable way.

CAPITALISM

The arms race as a process (i. e., "You threatened me, so I have to defend myself.") often has been cited as a major cause in provoking conflict, with the profit motive of private manufacturers assuming the function of a small spring which helps keep the balance wheel ticking. Another popular theory is that the profit motive is the mainspring which drives nations full speed into war. Marx, for example, held that war was simply the inevitable result of competing capitalists. Which capitalist state triumphed, was of no importance, he reasoned, for in the final revolutionary reaction, socialism would prevail. When that happened—when the ownership of the means of production finally was in the hands of the people—then war would cease.

Marx blames man's institutions—manmade structured attitudes—and not his inherently aggressive nature for the evil of war. And the institution that particularly concerns Marx is capitalism, the competition between ruling classes of one nation and ruling classes of another for raw materials and markets. The logical outcome of capitalism, Marx believes, is armed conflict. Thus, in Socialism and War Lenin states:

> We (socialists) understand that war cannot be abolished unless classes are abolished and socialism is created; and we also differ (from the bourgeois, pacifists, and the anarchists) in that we regard civil war, i.e., wars waged by the oppressed class, slaves against slaveowners, by serfs against landowners, and wage workers against the bourgeoisie, as fully legitimate, progressive, and necessary. (Lenin, p. 10, 1915; emphasis added.)

and further, he says:

> The manifesto on war that was unanimously adopted in Bade in 1912 had in view the very war between Britain, Germany, and their present allies that broke out in 1914. The manifesto openly declares that no plea of the interests of the people can justify such a war, waged "for the sake of the profits of the capitalists and the ambitions of dynasties" on the basis of the imperialist predatory policy of the great powers. (Lenin, p. 24, 1915; emphasis added.)

The premise that the greed of private enterprise is a root cause of war is widely held and is by no means confined to communist doctrine. Noel-Baker observed that "both the French and German General Staffs had great influence, often openly exercised, often clandestine, through their connections with powerful private arms interests and the organs of the press, radio, and cinema which these interests controlled." (Noel-Baker, 1937.) C.W. Mills noted that "... connections between economic conditions and war preparations are not obscure and hidden; they are publicly and regularly reported. And they are definitely among ... the causes of World War III." (Mills, 1958, p. 57.) Even President Eisenhower, himself a product of the military, warned of the "military-industrial complex" in his farewell address to the nation. If, for the Marxist-Leninists, capitalism is war's only cause, it must also be assigned at least a large share of the blame by those of other political and economic persuasions.

But economic motives are not the only cause of war; nor are they even the major factor. Tensions exist today along a 4,000 mile border between two great communist nations—the U.S.S.R. and the People's Republic of China—and war between them is not an impossibility. We shall see later, when we examine the scientific data, that the root causes of war go deeper than the greed and hunger for profit associated with capitalism.

NATIONALISM

If for Marx the evil spawner of war was capitalism, for others, the institution which initiates war's mischief and misery is the sovereign nation-state itself. This idea has been cited by many—from ancient philosopher to modern anthropologist—but nowhere is it more cogently expressed than by Emery Reves in his Anatomy of Peace. "Wars take place whenever and wherever non-integrated social units of equal sovereignty come into contact." (Reves, 1945, p. 121.) This is a simple, all-inclusive idea, whose sheer elegance is attractive. What is the logic behind this view? Since prehistoric times, man has struggled by means of physical violence to foray for food, to maintain order within his ranks, and to defend himself against those whom he perceives as enemies. Baboons defend the troop, their society; early man defended the tribe, his society; and modern man defends the nation-state, which he perceives as his society. Until there is some form of world government, the World Federalists maintain that mankind will continue to have wars. Certainly, their view has validity. But if only law and order were needed, why then have there been so many civil wars? Nationalism is a villain, according to a great deal of evidence, but again, it is not the _only_ villain.

INNATE AGGRESSION

All the theories discussed so far have been based upon man's institutions, formalized behaviour patterns, which take many shapes. But common to all these patterns is a factor that eventually must be confronted—man's aggressive behaviour. Every discussion about the causes of war arrives at the question, what makes man aggressive? Is it heredity? or environment? or both? If we could answer these questions, we might then learn to direct that nature toward more positive goals.

Overcoming man's aggressive—some would call it evil—basic nature has been the source material for most of the world's great religions. Christianity offers ample evidence of this. It presupposes that individual man has good innately within him and that he can rise above the baser elements—the original sin—within his make-up. "Love," said Christ, "is a leavening force," and in a sense many of Jesus' teachings suggest an arms race in microcosm—at the personal level—to which the solution is man's own "disarmament."

The creed of the pacifist and the advocate of unilateral disarmament is the discipline of nonviolence. Gandhi practiced it in India in his successful attempt to secure his country's independence from British rule. More recently, Martin Luther King, the American civil rights leader, used nonviolence in his quest to secure political and economic freedom for the Negro in the United States. But the inheritance of Gandhi's independence movement, following the partition of India and Pakistan, was violent civil strife which cost more than 800,000 lives; and pent-up emotions connected with the American civil rights movement could very well follow a similar pattern.

Two facets of the nonviolent ethic should be examined carefully. First, does the expression of love and nonviolence elicit a nonviolent response? And, secondly, do the followers of a religion, e.g., Christianity, actually follow their founder's ideal of replacing hatred with love? Regrettably, historical and scientific evidence suggests that the answer to both questions must be negative; love and nonviolence, it would seem, cannot be made the basis of a stable peace. Nominal Christians do not seem to have replaced hatred with love any more than non-Christians (indeed, even less than some non-Christians). Moreover, the results of laboratory experiments suggest that, even if church members returned good for evil, their sacrifice would be exploited often enough to make the technique of nonviolence an unreliable guarantor of peace.

But if the moral injunction to love your neighbour as yourself seems to be insufficient, why is that so? Is war a product of man himself—his inner nature—or of man's institutions? It is strange and unfortunate that, despite half a century of scientific inquiry and debate, this question is still unresolved. Many scientists believe that man's violence is at least partly instinctual. This view is cogently expressed by the psychiatrist, Joost A. M. Meerloo, who maintains that "... nature threatens man ... but often more overpowering are the dangers arising from man's inner world: man's instinctual drives, his destructiveness, his aggression, his will for power.... The aggressive, hostile man of the twentieth century, with his highly improved destructive fighting tools, is still, unconsciously, the primitive Neanderthal who is unsure of his neighbors' intentions." (Meerloo, 1961.) But many other scientists, the environmentalists, are equally sure that instinct plays no important part in man's adult behaviour. Ashley Montagu states: "It is probable that there is not an iota of innate hostile aggressiveness in human beings ... the contemporary practice is to assume that man has no instincts, and that virtually everything that he does as a human being which is not reflex he has to learn from other human beings." (Montagu, 1958.) In the same vein, Elton B. McNeil writes: "As the child's capacity for verbal, abstract, and symbolic responses increases, the comparison of animal and man no longer contains either truth or relevance." (McNeil, 1966.)

Certainly, such controversies and seemingly irreconcilable differences of opinion are not new to science. Physicists will recall the once bitter argument over the propagation of light. Huygens, the Dutch physicist, believed light was a wave motion and that this could account for the bending of light rays by a lens and for the reflection of light from a mirror. Newton, on the other hand, insisted that light was simply the emission of corpuscles, or particles, which would explain, he said, why light normally travels in straight lines and why white light is split up into a rainbow spectrum of colours by a prism, like the bevelled edge of a mirror. Largely because Newton's great authority supported the corpuscular theory, Huygens' alternative wave theory was "laid aside and neglected for over a century." (Cajori, 1929.) Indeed, the controversy surrounding these two seemingly opposing theories went unresolved until 1905 and the advent of Einstein's quantum theory of light. Both Huygens and Newton, of course, were right. We know now, thanks to Einstein, that light quanta, like all the fundamental particles of physics (electrons, protons, and photons, for example), must be regarded as obeying both the laws governing particles and those of wave motion. They bend under the influence of gravity (for light waves this bending is small); yet two beams can interfere with each other like the wakes of two ocean freighters.

Many scientists are convinced that the environment-versus-instinct conflict can be resolved similarly. They believe the ultimate answer will be that both instinct (or, better, basic drives) and environment motivate and stimulate us and that learning is largely the result of a cultural process controlled by our various institutions.

POPULATION, RACE, AND SOME OTHERS

In considering these single-cause theories of the origin of war, we have glossed over or ignored many other partial but significant perceptions. Among these are a host of tension-producing factors which many believe to be war's precipitants: population pressures, inequalities of wealth, differences of race, of language, and of religion. Some practical politicians and some political theorists would add to the foregoing list: political ideologies, territorial ambitions, and the struggle to maintain a "balance of power."

"Territorial competition is the basic concept of international relations," according to the economist, Kenneth Boulding (Boulding, 1966.) Love of excitement is cited by some, while yet other scholars believe war is caused by the famous or infamous leaders of history, such as Napoleon, Ghengis Khan, or Hitler.

The job at hand is to reconcile these widely held diverse views, if possible, or to offer a more credible alternative hypothesis. Not surprisingly, a vast number of research studies from different disciplines bear on the problem, and the most recent of these have a strong mathematical base. Together, these studies produce a jigsaw puzzle which, though the pieces have not all been turned up or put into place, at least begins to look like a picture. The players who have assembled the jigsaw, and who still argue over the pieces, include political scientists, zoologists, physicists, physicians, sociologists, and psychologists. Their common calling is a love of truth, devotion to the scientific method, and in many cases, the desire for a better world. Let's look at their evidence.

3 biological evidence

In Civilization and Its Discontents Freud stated that "... the tendency to aggression is an innate, independent, instinctual disposition in man ... constituting the most powerful obstacle to culture." (Freud, 1930.) And in an open letter to Albert Einstein in 1932, he remarked that " ... there is no likelihood of our being able to suppress humanity's aggressive tendencies ... what we may try is to divert it into a channel other than that of warfare.... it may not be utopian to hope that these two factors, the cultural attitude and the justified dread of the consequences of a future war, may result within a measurable time in putting an end to the waging of war ... whatever fosters the growth of culture works at the same time against war." (Freud, 1933, p. 808.)

But what fosters the growth of culture? On the psychological side," Freud said, "two of the most important phenomena of culture are, first a strengthening of the intellect which tends to master our instinctive life, and secondly, an introversion of the aggressive impulse ... " (Freud, 1933, p. 810.) To Freud, it was apparent that man's innate tendencies are similar to those of fish, birds, and primates. For example, modern awareness of the power of the sexual urge in man and its repression and diversion to the subconscious is due largely to Freud's genius. But while aggression and sex were perhaps his two major concerns, other apparent urges did not escape Freud's attention. "I once interested myself," he commented, "in the peculiar fact that people whose territories are adjacent, and are otherwise closely related, are always at feud with and ridiculing each other." (Freud, 1930, p. 788.)

A half century after Freud's birth, Vienna produced a second great experimental physician, Konrad Lorenz. But while Freud had been fascinated by people—whether Polynesians, early Sumatrans, or modern Europeans—Lorenz was concerned with wild animal life—from stickleback fish to graylag geese to wolves, dogs, and primates. Both men focused their studies primarily on instincts. Freud dealt at length with aggression in man and Lorenz, with aggression in other animals. But while the parallels in their interests and careers are noteworthy, their approaches were entirely different. Of Freud, Lorenz once wrote: "Discussions of his theories of motivation revealed unexpected correspondences between the findings of psychoanalysis and behavioral physiology, which seemed all the more significant because of the differences in approach, method, and above all inductive basis between the two disciplines." (Lorenz, 1966, p. x.)

This chapter will deal with certain instincts or innate tendencies in animals; later chapters will show how closely these parallel certain tendencies in man.

AGGRESSION

There are, according to Lorenz, four fundamental instincts which condition the life of most species; flight (or fear), fight (or aggression), sexuality, and hunger. Sometimes one instinct is dominant, sometimes another, but more often several are in sharp conflict.

How can Lorenz be certain that the four instincts are really separate and distinct from one another? One technique used by Lorenz and other naturalists is observation or, more explicitly, the technique of motivation and factor analysis. This analysis has sometimes produced unexpected discoveries. Oehlert, for example, in studying cichlids (fish) was confronted by a provocative question. Since male and female cichlids of a certain species were apparently identical, the puzzled investigator wondered how mating cichlids overcame the problem of sex recognition. Interestingly, Oehlert found that the lack of a certain behaviour pattern was their most important clue.

> In the male, the motivations of flight and of sexuality cannot be mixed. If the male has even the slightest fear of his partner, his sexuality is completely extinguished; in the female, there is the same relationship between aggression and sexuality; if she is so little in awe of her partner that her aggression is not entirely suppressed, she does not react to him sexually at all. She becomes a Brunhilde and attacks him the more ferociously the more potentially ready she is for

> sexual relations, that is, the nearer she is to spawning, in respect to her ovarian and hormonal state. (Lorenz, 1966, p. 102.)

The point at issue here is not the sex life of cichlids, interesting as that may be, but that the three drives, aggression, fear, and sex, can so neatly be disentangled in at least one species. The tendency to aggression, for a cichlid, can be proven to be an "innate, independent, instinctual disposition," to use the words Freud applied to man. But the cichlid is not alone in having a disposition for aggression; Lorenz and his co-workers found it in many other species.

By aggression we are speaking of the fighting instinct in animals, including man, which is directed against members of the same species. By this definition, a species is not aggressive towards another species; a hawk is not aggressive towards a mouse. "What directly threatens the existence of an animal species is never the eating enemy but the competitor." (Lorenz, 1966, p. 25.) In a balanced state of nature it is the competitors which strive after the same food. "Never have I seen fish of two different species attacking each other," Lorenz maintains, "even if both are highly aggressive by nature." (Lorenz, 1966, p. 11; emphasis added.) When predators attack their natural prey, the prey (unless cornered) takes to flight, not fight.

TERRITORY

Why are members of a given species (hawks to hawks, rats to rats, man to man) aggressive towards one another? It is the natural outgrowth of competition over territory, says Lorenz, for territory is all-important to animals. Territory endows its owner with a perpetual chance for food and with a place to build a nest. The competitive process thus causes a mutual repulsion among animals of the same species. Like air filling a vacuum, they will spread out to occupy all of the available space; they share the available food and nesting sites. Since animals of different species do not normally require the same food, or nesting locations, there is no competition for these things among them. Although a robin, a squirrel, and a woodpecker will coexist on the same tree, two male robins (or squirrels, or woodpeckers) will not tolerate each other's presence.

Moreover, the amount of territory an animal possesses varies according to its readiness to fight competitors:

> In nearing the center of the territory the aggressive urge increases in geometric ratio to the decrease in distance from this center. This increase in aggression is so great it compensates for all differences ever to be found in adult, sexually-mature animals of a species.
>
> During an encounter (between two animals), the inertia of reaction of both animals leads to that phenomenon which always occurs when a time lag enters into a self-regulating process—an oscillation. The courage of the fugitive returns as he nears his own headquarters, while that of the pursuer sinks in proportion to the distance covered in enemy territory. (Lorenz, 1966, p. 164.)

Lorenz describes how through a series of natural events, the territorial borders seesawed back and forth in his aquarium. First, the stronger male (A) took possession of most of the tank; then the weaker male (B) fought back and recovered a more rightful share. Subsequently, A paired, and the resulting pair resumed the larger territory; but when B took a mate as well, the border was again in the middle of the tank. At this point pair A spawned, and since their fighting power diminished, they lost a large portion of their territory; finally, pair B spawned, too, and the old balance was restored.

Conflicts over territory also take place between groups of animals of the same species. In 1950 it was demonstrated by J. Steiniger, and independently by Eibl-Eibesfeldt, that brown rats and house mice will not tolerate colonies other than their own. Within the blood group there is a sort of impersonal bond of affection, but for other groups there is death and massacre.

On the small North Sea island of Norderoog, Steiniger found that the ground was divided between a small number of rat clans separated by a strip of about 50 yards of "no rat's land" where fights were constantly taking place (Eibl-Eibesfeldt.) This perpetual warfare between large neighbouring families of rats seems to exert a powerful selection process in the direction of an ever-increasing ability to fight. Within the large clans, themselves, however, there are no serious fights, even when they comprise dozens of animals. While the rats do not know each other "personally," as jackdaws, geese, and monkeys do, they recognize each other by the clan smell.

(Lorenz, 1966.) But when a rat enters another clan's territory, or is put there by an experimenter, his death is a foregone conclusion and in short order he is literally torn to pieces. Steiniger relates how he placed individual brown rats from a dozen localities into the same large enclosure:

> At first the individual animals seemed afraid of each other; they were not in an aggressive mood, but they bit each other if they met by chance, particularly if two were driven towards each other along one side of the enclosure, so that they collided at speed. However, they became really aggressive only when they began to settle and take possession of territories ... Even in the 102 square yard enclosure, two or three weeks sufficed for one pair to kill all the other residents, ten to fifteen strong adult rats. (Lorenz, 1966, p. 158.)

Another example of territorial aggression in animal society also illustrates the dominant role of the leader. While rhesus monkeys cannot compare with rats in ferocity, they probably exceed most other animals in the extent of their aggressiveness. Describing a now-famous experiment in which C. R. Carpenter settled 350-odd rhesus monkeys from India on a 36-acre island off the coast of Puerto Rico, Robert Ardrey writes:

> Arriving at Santiago Island they entered what any primate must regard as monkey Utopia. No leopards haunted their nocturnal

> hours, or pythons their day-time excursions. There was food in abundance distributed daily and evenly by the island caretakers. Yet within a year the whole monkey community divided itself into social groups, each holding and defending a preset territory and living in permanent hostility with its neighbors. (Ardrey, 1961, p. 44.)

While studying his various groups, Carpenter made an astonishing discovery—one of the groups embarked on conquest:

> Group number one infringed on its neighbors—and got away with it. Daily, regularly, group one made its feeding excursions onto the territories of not just one but five neighboring societies. Group one was opposed ... by the injured societies. There was no weakness in the opposition. But group one by some mysterious power broke that most fundamental of animal laws, that the home team wins. In this case the home teams, all of them, lost; and group one had its way on opposition territory. (Ardrey, 1961, p. 107.)

Group one had as its leader a male of almost unbelievable dominance, and his presence in his group seemed to communicate to the others the resources of his nature. When Carpenter removed this master monkey from group one, it "immediately fell back to its own territory," not once commiting a single act of trespass. When Carpenter ended the master monkey's exile, however, group one unhesitatingly "returned to its field of conquest." (Ardrey, 1961, p. 102.)

It has frequently been suggested that only certain animals have territorial instincts; among those which are thought to lack such instincts are nomadic animals like the wolf. Of considerable interest then is this description from Farley Mowat's delightful and factual story of the Canadian northland, Never Cry Wolf.

> The territory owned by my wolf family comprised more than a hundred square miles, bounded on one side by a river but otherwise not delimited by geographical features. Nevertheless there *were* boundaries; clearly indicated in wolfish fashion.
>
> Anyone who has observed a dog doing his neighborhood rounds and leaving his personal mark on each convenient post will have already guessed how the wolves marked out their property. (Mowat, 1963, p. 59.)

Mowat describes how, in wolf-like fashion, he marked out a 3-acre estate of his own after consuming several quarts of tea. But even this alien introduction did not form a subject of disagreement. The wolf merely sought out each boundary marker and in turn placed his mark on the outside of each clump of grass or stone.

STATUS AND LEADERSHIP

How can large groups of fish, or fowl, or beasts live together in peace when each individual is by nature aggressive towards others of the same species? Surviving species must owe their continued existence, at least in part, to the development of other instincts to protect individuals within the group. Three of these protective instincts, according to Lorenz, are status, love, and the inhibiting mechanism. In later chapters, it will be seen that the first two appear to exist in man.

Status, the pecking-order system, reduces conflict to a minimum by insuring that each member of the group acts aggressively towards the next lowest member in the pecking order. Lorenz explains:

> Do animals thus know each other among themselves? They certainly do, though many learned animal psychologists have doubted the fact and indeed denied it categorically. Nevertheless, I can assure you, every single jackdaw of my colony knew each of the others by sight. This can be convincingly demonstrated by the existence of an order of rank, known to animal psychologists as the "pecking order."
>
> The rank order disputes in a jackdaw colony differ in one important way from those in the poultry yard ... in the jackdaw colony, those of the higher orders, particularly the despot himself, are not aggressive towards the birds that stand far beneath them; it is only in their relations towards their immediate inferiors that they are constantly irritable.... Thus a high-caste jackdaw, particularly the despot himself, acts regularly on chivalrous principles—where there's an unequal fight he always takes the weaker side.

> Since the major quarrels are mostly concerned with nesting sites (in nearly all other cases, the weaker bird withdraws without a struggle), this propensity of the strong male jackdaw ensures an active protection of the nests of the lower members of the colony. (Lorenz, 1966, p. 147.)

The responsibility of leadership has its advantages in the animal as well as in the human world. With leadership goes prestige. Robert M. Yerkes made the remarkable observation that chimpanzees, animals well known to be capable of learning by imitation, copy only higher-ranking members of their species. The skills of lower-ranking individuals, no matter how well trained they may be by the experimenter, are ignored by their higher ranking fellows. (Lorenz, 1966, p. 46.) No skill would seem to be more appropriate to survival than recognition of the enemy. Yet this skill, which is innate to many animals, must be taught to some. Learned through experience? No, imprinted on young minds by their elders. For some animals, as for all humans, "prejudice" must be taught. Writes Lorenz:

> I do not know whether I have made it quite clear how very remarkable all of this is: an animal, which does not know its enemy by innate instinct, is informed by older and more experienced fellow-members of its species who or what is to be feared as hostile. This is true tradition, the handing-down of personally-acquired knowledge from one generation to another.... On the appearance of an enemy, as yet unknown to the

> young, an old guide jackdaw needs only to give one significant "rattle," and at once the young birds have formed a mental picture associating the warning with this particular enemy. (Lorenz, 1952, p. 144.)

LOVE

One of the strangest and one of the newest instincts of the animal world is the personal bond of friendship. Cichlids have it, graylag geese have it, and mammals generally have it in abundance. It should not be confused with the reproductive urge (though in the species concerned it generally exists between mates), for it can bind the whole group or, in some cases, knit together only two animals of the same sex. Decoding nature's processes is often tedious, frequently fascinating, but rarely more so than in the discovery of the origin of this bond. For love generally has been an outgrowth of aggression, and its step-by-step development was deduced by observing species at each step along the way, just as the evolution of stars was deduced by observing the differences in radiation from stars of different age.

Among mammals, rites of friendship are the rule; we will touch on only one species, but as already noted, it is one of the most aggressive—rats.

> Within the pack there is no real fighting, at the most there is slight friction, boxing with the fore-paws or kicking with the hind paws, but never biting; and within the pack there is no individual distance. On the contrary, rats are con-

> tact animals ... they like touching each other. The ceremony of friendly contact is the so-called "creeping under" which is performed particularly by young animals, while larger animals show their sympathy for smaller ones by creeping over them.... (Lorenz, 1966, p. 160.)

Two points about love need to be stressed. The personal bond, an individual friendship, is found only in animals with a highly developed urge for aggression; in fact, the more aggressive the particular animal or species, the firmer the bond. Lorenz claims that while personal friendship, or love, is a firm independent instinct it is millions of years younger than aggression, for "a son can't be older than his father." (Lorenz, 1966, p. 217.) He suggests that aggression can exist without love, but that no species has been found to have love without aggression.

Social animals exhibit specific rites of friendship which tend to unite the group; they also show definite acts of friendship particularly when one member is distressed. Lilly has described a dolphin which had been kept in a cold tank for so long that he had become too paralyzed to swim. The keeper then transferred him to a warm-water tank.

> As soon as he was put into the tank with the other two dolphins, he emitted the distress call. Immediately the other dolphins came and lifted his head up so that his blowhole was pushed up out of the water. He breathed and went down. A lot of whistling and twittering went on among the three of them. The two others now changed their tac-

tics and instead of swimming under his head to lift it up they swam under his ano-genital region. As they passed underneath, their dorsal fins raked the very sensitive external openings of this region. The contact caused a reflex contraction downward of the powerful flukes, which forced the animal upward to the life-giving air. They kept this tactic up for several hours. (Lilly, 1961.)

Vetulani observed another example of animal co-operation during the course of experiments with mice in groups and in isolation. Some of his mice had lesions on the skin which they treated by licking. If these were in the head region they could only be treated by another individual. Vetulani noticed that when isolated mice with lesions were brought together for further experimentation, the wounds were soon cured by their new nest mates. (Allee, 1938.)

INHIBITIONS

Individual deer, doves, or rabbits seek safety through flight and escape, whether the attacker is their natural enemy or a stronger more aggressive member of their own kind. The social animals, the goose, monkey, and baboon, make use of rank order and love to protect themselves from their own species. But what of the raven or the wolf? What defence have these creatures against their own when their beak or fangs can kill a fellow member in a single blow? For such killers who live together in groups, nature has evolved (as she must have for the species to survive) yet another device—the inhibiting mechanism.

To see how the inhibiting mechanism operates let us consider the wolf, for in few species is an instinct more wonderfully developed and so sure of preventing slaughter. A wolf that offers its unprotected neck to its adversary will never be bitten seriously. This strange inhibition from biting persists, however, only so long as the defeated wolf maintains his attitude of humility. (Lorenz, 1952, p. 186.) Key to the performance is the instinctive submissive gesture which triggers off the inhibition. Predatory birds like the raven offer to their adversary at the moment of submission, the most vulnerable part of their bodies, that part against which every killing attack is inevitably directed, the area at the base of the skull. Thus supplicated, the victorious bird, like the wolf, is unable to make the fatal blow. (Lorenz, 1952, p. 193.)

As we go down the scale of "deadliness," in the animal world, the submissive gesture is both less sudden and less sure. The female baboon, when afraid of a threatening male, makes a habit of "presenting." By thus seeking to inflame his sexual urge she apparently drains away his aggression. Katharina Heinroth describes a female baboon who, upon entering a strange room, "presented" her behind to each chair in turn, for to her the strange chairs were a threat. Oddly enough, at the end of an all-male fight, the losing male baboon will "present" himself to the victor. Rather than an invitation to homosexuality, the submissive gesture serves as a truce flag, for the action arouses in the attacker a nonaggressive tendency which competes with and inhibits the aggressiveness that is present. (Lorenz, 1966, p. 136.) By performing either juvenile or sexual patterns, a submissive animal arouses parental or sexual responses in the aggressor and in this way stops the attack. (Carthy and Ebling, 1964, p. 37.)

To complete the picture, it is necessary to describe what happens to animals when nature's protection is removed. What, for example, befalls animals which normally flee from an aggressor when they are in captivity? Their fate is a frightful one, for the aggressor has his way unchecked. Turtledoves in captivity will peck one another unmercifully until the weaker one, unable to escape, dies from loss of blood and exhaustion. But this example of death occurring between two members of the same species is the exception. In general, intraspecies aggression is rarely fatal, for nature has provided a sufficient number of built-in checks.

Does man have inhibitory mechanisms against killing his own kind? We do not know for sure. Lorenz implies that man does have a natural though possibly rather weak repugnance to killing man when he asks the reader to "try—only in imagination, of course—to kill in succession a lettuce, a fly, a frog, a guinea pig, a cat, a dog, and finally a chimpanzee.... The degree of _inhibition_ against killing each one of these beings is a very precise measure of the considerably different values that we cannot help attributing to lower and higher forms of life. To any man who finds it equally easy to chop up a live dog and a live lettuce I would recommend suicide at his earliest convenience!" Lorenz, 1966, p. 226.)

A final important example of unleashed aggression should be cited. So strong is intra-species aggression in animals in confined spaces that its threshold easily can be lowered; that is, in the absence of suitable competitors, the urge is often "displaced." In aquarium cichlids an apparent "damming up" of aggression, which under normal circumstances would be directed towards territorial neighbours, can very easily lead to the male fish's actually killing his mate. He "needs" to vent his aggression on someone, and in the absence of natural neighbours she becomes a scapegoat. (Lorenz, 1966, p. 54.) In this displacement response cichlids are not alone, for other caged animals exhibit the same behaviour. And, as we shall see, human societies also seem sometimes to "displace" their aggression.

4 anthropological evidence

The psychologist Elton B. McNeil claims that we can learn little about ourselves by observing animals. "It is wildly improbable," he said, "that the anthill, beehive, or monkey colony has much to teach modern, interplanetary, atomic man.... Man's animal nature is a feeble excuse for violence...." (McNeil, 1966, p. 151.) Most scientists, however, are less scornful of man's animal past; they regard it rather as part of the total picture. Thus, anthropologist Santiago Genovés queries: "How can we be sure that human culture and human intelligence, which separate us from the animals, do not play as great a part in human aggression as any instincts that we may have inherited from our animal origins?" The pioneer ethologist Nikolaas Tinbergen puts the nature-nurture argument in even clearer perspective: "... human aggression results from the cultural reinforcement of a biological heritage that man shares with the animals." (Genovés, 1970, p. 74.)

Is man's animal nature, indeed, only part of a dim, distant heritage which has little relevance today? While this seems unlikely, unless an evolutionary continuity can be shown to link animal behaviour with that of man, the biological evidence of the previous chapter is only as interesting as Kipling's Jungle Books or Just So Stories and, for practical purposes, just as relevant. It is one thing to demonstrate that animal behaviour is primarily instinctive; it is quite another to prove that the vestige of instinct has been passed along from lower animals to man through a natural selection process.

Evidence to this effect can be drawn from several sources. An important body of data are the systematically analyzed historical facts about modern wars compiled by Lewis Fry Richardson. (Richardson, 1960a.) As a supplement to the Richardson work, there are a variety of recent statistical surveys and laboratory experiments. Relating these facts about modern wars to the animal data are two anthropological studies. The first concerns our little-known forebear Australopithicus africanus (Ardrey, 1961); and the second analyzes the wars of 50 primitive tribes (Naroll, 1966.) An analysis of these studies indicates that man follows the same aggressive behaviour patterns as do his evolutionary forebears. (See chapters 12 and 13.)

AUSTRALOPITHECUS AFRICANUS

The biological evidence in respect to aggression so far discussed has been based on observations of the lower animals. With African man we must depend on indirect evidence deduced from bones left in caves more than half a million years ago. The evidence is highly significant, because Australopithecus africanus is half-ape and half-man and, therefore, may be the last animal below man on the evolutionary ladder. Between Australopithecus africanus (southern ape) and true man the size of the brain is the only significant difference; man's is larger. The southern ape walked erectly or nearly so, was an omnivore like man and his teeth were nearly like ours.

The most remarkable characteristic of Australopithecus africanus for the purpose of studying war is that this creature killed his prey, not with his fangs (he had none) nor with his claws (they were inadequate) but with weapons, chiefly the humerus bone of the antelope. Thus, man was not the first creature to use weapons for food and defence. Complete documentation of this fact can be found in African Genesis, in which Robert Ardrey, a playwright who over a decade ago turned to the study of man, defends the scientific evidence of Raymond Dart, a South African physician who became an anthropologist. In a limestone cave in South Africa, Dr. Dart had found some fossil remains which looked distinctly human, indeed like those of a human child. Of Dart's conclusions, Ardrey wrote:

> On the basis of many an anatomical diagnosis, Dart projected the adult creature as being four feet tall and weighing ninety pounds, with a brain about as large as that of a gorilla. He concluded that his infant's baby canine teeth would be replaced by mature canine teeth no larger than human. Out of his total anatomical diagnosis emerged a simple definition that still fits all of the hundred-odd individual australopithecines

known today: they were creatures lacking the fighting teeth of apes, who combined man's erect carriage with the ape's small brain.

To his anatomical description Dart added his conclusion that Australopithecus africanus had been a carnivore. Evidence for his revolutionary conclusion was of three sorts. First, in the arid environment of the Taungs site there could have been no sufficient source of nourishment for a fruit-eating, vegetarian ape. Secondly, there was the matter of the associated fossils. The deposit resembled that of a kitchen midden such as is left behind by primitive man. If the fossilized bones were not the remains of animals brought to the cave as food, then how did they get there?

But it was Dart's third line of evidence that concerns us most deeply as a clue to our human ancestry. The teeth of Australopithecus africanus are all but indistinguishable from our own. They are small. The enamel is not thick. The shape and arrangement are like ours. And the crowns like our own are totally inadequate for the endless grinding and munching of a vegetarian creature who must gain from low-calorie foodstuffs sufficient daily nourishment to support a fair-sized body. All evidence combined to indicate that Dart's little infant found in a lime deposit on the edge of an African desert had once been a member of a meat-eating family of primates....

(Furthermore,) John Robinson's microscopic studies of Australopithecus teeth confirm ... the teeth of africanus are as smooth as a leopard's. (Ardrey, 1961, pp. 176 and 181.)

But weapons? Of the many pieces of evidence assembled by Ardrey, the following are pertinent:

Dart (1949) described the fractured skulls of certain baboons found at Makapan, Sterkfontein, and Taungs, as the consequence of assault by a weapon. The peculiar nature of many of the injuries suggested to him that the weapon had been the humerus bone of the antelope. Six years later, after an analysis of 4,560 fossil fragments developed from the Makapan breccia, he found that 518 were portions of the bone in question.

The baboon injuries consisted of a double-depressed area which could be caused only by the distal (elbow) end of the humerus bone. The proximal (shoulder) end could not cause it. Among the total humerus bone fragments Dart found 336 distal ends, 33 proximal ends.

In his analysis of the 3,500 antelope fragments (discounting loose teeth) Dart uses 38 anatomical classifications, by body part, each of which is divided into four categories determined by the size of the animal. The 3,500 fragments are therefore divided into 152 brackets. Five of these 152 brackets contribute twenty-two per cent of all the remains. They are the humerus bone distal end (238), metacarpal bone distal end (135), horn core (122), and lower jaw (98), all of the medium antelope. Again we have a statistical distribution that could not occur except through

> some agency of selection. (Ardrey, 1961, p. 294.)

Some scholars have suggested that the scavanging hyena, not the semi-human creature, had collected the bones; but the case for the hyena does not stand up nearly so well as the case for Australopithecus africanus, as documented by Ardrey. Australopithecus africanus, he concluded, was a meat-eating animal ill-equipped by nature to satisfy his normal diet without the use of a weapon. He derived that weapon from his prey, the antelope, and often used it against another prey, the baboon.

We know nothing more about Australopithecus africanus, this primate ancestor, than that he used a bone club to kill his prey including the baboon. The lime caves of the South African veldt tell us nothing at all about his aggression or about his activities toward his own kind; also we have no idea of the size of his normal group.

One point about Australopithecus africanus is worth emphasizing. If weapons "came down" to man from a creature who was only partly human, can the urge to fashion tools and weapons now be thought of as innate? Moreover, if man's preoccupation with weapons is a deep-seated motivation, and if there has not been time for the evolution of the kind of strong compensatory inhibiting mechanism possessed by most other predators, man's aggression is a more dangerous aggression than that of other animals which live in groups.

An interesting sidelight on the subject of fossils is the discovery in 1927 of 11 skull caps of Peking man, neatly buried in a row (Coon, 1965.) If this discovery does not prove that early man was dangerously aggressive, it is worthy of speculation at least.

If the fossil remains of Australopithecus africanus tell us nothing definitive about the fighting habits of our forebears, written accounts of the warring habits of primitive tribes certainly do. For primitive tribesmen used weapons extensively for fighting their fellow man—their arsenal included spears and clubs, bows, rocks, and blow-pipes. A study of such tribes was recently made by the anthropologist Raoul Naroll.

PRIMITIVE TRIBES

Naroll took as his starting point four hypotheses about war, which here are condensed into three:

(1a) The Arms Race: Wars are caused by armaments, since each side strives without limit for military supremacy.

(1b) Deterrence: Wars are prevented by armaments, since rationally an enemy can perceive that he will not gain from war.

(2) Cultural selectivity: Wars are necessary for a society to survive, since the strongest culture will outlast the weak.

(3) Cultural exchange: Wars are less likely if people from both sides get to know one another better, since fear and suspicion of the stranger are the basis of war.

To test these hypotheses, Naroll compared selected characteristics of 50 primitive societies from around the world. All but one of the tribes were illiterate. The samples ranged, geographically, from the Hottentots and Mongos of Africa to the Chukchi of Siberia, the Gond of India, the Land Dyak of Malaya, the Cheyenne of North America, and the Arucanians of South America. The data for the study were drawn mainly from the Human Relations Area File, and the time period studied was most often the century preceding colonial conquest.

What did Naroll discover? For one thing he concluded that those societies which expected great things from war—territory, revenge, booty, or prestige—went to war most often. In technical terms this means there was a strong positive correlation between two variables, expectation of gain from war and frequency of war (See Figure 1). There was also a strong positive correlation between high expectations and readiness for war, readiness meaning that the tribes had some fortifications built and some warriors armed at all times. There was, however, only a moderately positive correlation between readiness for war and frequency of war, but this finding is fairly indeterminate, for one cannot be sure whether readiness for war is the cause of war, or conversely, whether frequent wars have caused the tribes to be more prepared. The findings do suggest, though, the "power of positive thinking," for those cultures with high expectations of gain from war are both better armed and fight more often.

In short, the findings give no support to the deterrence hypothesis—that arms prevent wars—since readiness for war correlated positively with frequency. The findings, on the contrary, give support for the arms race hypothesis—that wars are caused by war preparations themselves—though the correlation was not very strong.

Another part of the study was more fruitful. The

effect of warfare on the various societies was measured in terms of territorial change, which was indicated by two measures: growth (total positive change) and instability (total positive and negative change). Territorial growth, it is assumed, is correlated positively with the survival of a culture. Growth alone, Naroll reasons, is an insufficient measure of cultural survival; stability too is important, for "the society that keeps out of war as much as possible and avoids both gains and losses of territory may be the society most likely to survive."

Analysis of the 50 societies produced the following figures: 21 tribes showed no territorial change during the period recorded. Of the 29 that did have changes in territory, only three experienced the change peacefully. It follows then that territorial change is almost always brought about by warfare and has a strong positive correlation with frequency of war.

But is this a measure of growth, defined as good for the tribe in question, or simply a measure of instability caused, perhaps, by warfare itself? The analysis suggests that it is both, because readiness for war has a moderate positive correlation with both territorial growth and territorial instability. But territorial instability has a strong positive correlation with military expectations. So an interesting possibility is suggested by Naroll: Tribal lands are often the stakes of warfare, and not just a by-product of conflict.

Since territorial growth (assumed to be positively correlated with survival) and readiness for war are positively related, some support seems to be given to hypothesis 2 (i.e., that war is believed necessary for the survival of a culture), at least for the 50 primitive tribes that were studied. But territorial instability (assumed to be negatively correlated with survival) is also positively correlated with readiness for war, thus no conclusions can properly be drawn with respect to readiness for war and survival of a culture.

Survival of a culture may involve the civilian organization as much as or more than the military organization of a primitive society. The anthropologist Walter Goldschmidt has suggested that while the Zulu conquests in Africa were made possible by the development of a strong military organization, "the failure to supply adequate institutional mechanisms for widespread military conquest prevented the establishment of a large-scale social order, and a Zulu empire was never created. The Incas of Peru (on the other hand) were aware of this problem and recognized the social systems of conquered territories in such a way as to fit them into the basic pattern, though they changed native custom as little as possible." (Goldschmidt, 1959, p. 129.)

Naroll measured cultural exchange by three pieces of data: subsidies between tribes, trade, and traffic in women, including slaves and wives. When these data were subjected to analysis, hypothesis 3 was found to be as invalid as hypothesis 1b. Naroll regretfully concludes that his comparisons "show no significant relationships at all between the frequency of war and these three measures of peaceful intercourse."

The results of this study may not be completely convincing because of the assumptions regarding territorial change and survival of a society, but they are nonetheless valuable when considered with the research of other disciplines.

Figure 1

CORRELATIONS BETWEEN FREQUENCY, EXPECTATIONS AND READINESS FOR WAR, AND TERRITORIAL CHANGE FOR 50 PRIMITIVE SOCIETIES

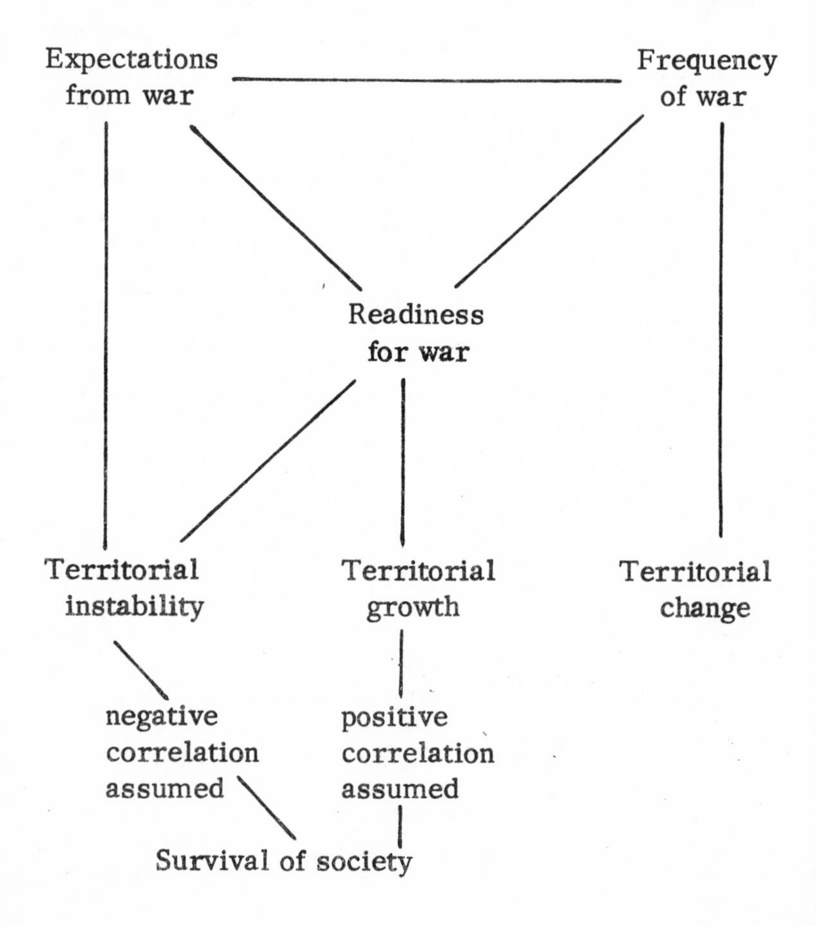

5 historical evidence

MODERN WARS

If a man from Mars were to study transportation on Earth, he might begin with the following statistical observations: People seem to travel in a variety of machines having some or all of these characteristics—wheels, an engine, wings, propellers, a set of controls, and some sort of body to hold all the parts together. As his studies proceeded, the Martian might sort these parts into several kinds of machines: One group apparently travels only on land and has a body, wheels, an engine, and a set of controls; another group, used for traveling on water, has a body, a propeller, an engine and a set of controls; a third group, used for flying through the air, is characterized by a body, wheels, a propeller, an engine, a set of controls, and wings. In a sense, this is simply a correlation analysis, for the probabilities are that if certain characteristics are present the vehicle will be used in a certain way. What this analysis does not explain is <u>how</u> the machines work and whether the various parts are either <u>necessary</u> of <u>sufficient.</u>

To understand how the vehicles work, one must look into the dynamics of the system. When the engine is filled with gasoline (a component overlooked by our friend from Mars) and some of the controls are adjusted, the engine is able to turn the wheels (if the machine is a car) and cause the vehicle to move. It may not move in the right direction, however, and its speed could be quite frightening. But when other controls are adjusted, the machine may be brought under control. Although the dynamics of the boat and the airplane will have much in common with the car, in certain important respects the boat and plane must be treated as quite different vehicles.

Unlike the man from Mars who looked at transportation on Earth from only one point of view—statistical—Lewis Richardson of England, who might well be called the father of mathematical peace research, looked at war from two points of view—the statistical and the dynamic. His two major works, written in 1947 and 1950 and published posthumously in 1960, stand as giant landmarks in a little-charted corner of the scientific world.

In Statistics of Deadly Quarrels he listed all the characteristics or "symptoms" of war which he thought conceivably useful and assigned these characteristics, where appropriate, to more than 300 wars which took place from 1820 to 1949, along with precise statements of each war's apparent causes. In these wars, Christians attacked Moslems, Protestants opposed Catholics, capitalists fought communists, pink-skinned people struggled against brown-skinned, brown-skinned clashed with black. Wars occurred between nations of equal size and power, small nations battled large, and groups of people within nations took up arms against other groups of their own nationality, sometimes to the point of genocide and extinction.

Man surely can be said to be a fighting animal and any adequate theory of the causes of war must certainly take account of the segment of history on which Richardson focuses. It is of interest that Quincy Wright, whose own monumental work (Wright, 1942) in some ways anticipated Richardson, had this to say in the foreword to Statistics of Deadly Quarrels: "One of the editors (Wright) made a study of war in 1942 from a background of legal, historical, and political study very different from that of Richardson. The comparison of conclusions, indicated in the footnotes, shows few inconsistencies, though Richardson's method often made the proof more convincing." (Richardson, 1960[a], p. viii.)

Statistics of Deadly Quarrels lists most of the fatal quarrels which occurred in the world from 1820 to 1949, arranged according to magnitude. Thus at the top of the list are World Wars I and II, each with a death toll of over 10 million people. A group of seven wars are next down the list, each with a death toll of from 300 thousand to three million persons: The Taiping Rebellion, 1851-64; North American Civil War, 1861-65; Great War in La Plata, 1865-70; Sequel to the Bolshevik Revolution, 1918-20; First Chinese-Communist War, 1927-36; Spanish Civil War, 1936-39; and Communal riots in the Indian peninsula, 1946-48. That is followed by a group of 20 fatal quarrels each involving 30 thousand to 300 thousand dead. The fourth group of 67 wars involve fatal casualties of three thousand to 30 thousand. Wars in these four groups are all separately identifiable, and, Richardson has reason to believe, are recorded fairly accurately and completely.

The next group—300 to 3,000 killed—totals 209 separate conflicts, but since according to Richardson its completeness is open to question, it is not used for some of the analyses. Fatal quarrels in the three to 30 and 30 to 300 ranges fall in the category of insurrections, riots and raids; only a total estimate of their number is given, using as references statistics from such sources as Banditry in Manchoukuo or Gang Warfare in Chicago. For murders and homicides, range one to three, figures are more readily available from police records of each country.

From a statistical analysis of these figures, Richardson is able to conclude that there is no evidence "of any general trend towards more or fewer quarrels of magnitude 2.5 to 4.5" (Richardson, 1960[a], p. 141) throughout the period studied. Designation of war magnitude, it should be noted, is based on the logarithm (to the base 10) of the number killed. Thus, 10,000,000 killed is magnitude 7; 1,000 is magnitude 3; while a single murder is magnitude 0. Magnitudes 2.5 and 4.5 are 316 and 3160 dead, respectively. It is a convenient system and we shall use it throughout this book.

What of variations in total killed as between murders and great wars? The figures are given in Table 1.

But while perhaps interesting in themselves these general trend statistics tell us little about the causes or correlates of conflict. To explore these in a systematic way Richardson broke his war data down into definite groups of belligerents. Thus the Seven weeks War of 1866 (40,000 killed, or magnitude 4.6) lists Prussians and Italians along the top and Austrians, Bavarians, Saxons, and Hanoverians down the side. In this case, the Prussians fought all four groups listed, while the Italians only fought the Austrians. Each pair of belligerents is further described. Fifty-nine symbols are available in the notation used by Richardson but only the most significant are mentioned here.

Table 1

TOTAL NUMBER OF PERSONS WHO DIED BECAUSE OF QUARRELS
(126 YEARS FROM A. D. 1820 to 1945)
(Richardson, 1960[a], p. 153)

Magnitude of fatal quarrel	7	6	5	4	3	2	1	0
No. of deaths in millions*	36	6.7	3.4	0.7	0.3	0.4	2.2	9.7

* Over the 126-year period 1.6 percent died from deadly quarrels.

Did the belligerents have a common mother tongue; similar or different religion or philosophy; similar or different bodily characteristics; similar or different customs as to dress? Perhaps they shared a common government for x years, indicating the quarrel was a civil war? held similar or different views on degree of personal liberty; had intermingled on the same territory up to the time the conflict began—one kind of civil war. Did one side habitually obey the other; wish to acquire territory from the other; or was it on the average evidently richer?

Richardson used his historic data to deduce evidence of man's war-like nature. He wanted to discover if it is a universal drive, or has been confined to certain cultures or areas of the world. Has language or religion an influence on the likelihood of war? How does economics affect man's behaviour? These are only a few of the questions this major study attempted to answer.

To illustrate how Richardson used his basic historical facts to reach definite conclusions, here is one of his analyses in detail. The question asked is whether all nations during the period 1820 to 1949 were equally likely to engage in war, or whether the activity of war was more characteristic of some nations than of others. And if it was, why was this so?

IS WAR-MAKING A NATIONAL CHARACTERISTIC?

Richardson began his analysis with an observation: "The Dumbarton Oaks Conference proposed in 1944 that membership of the United Nations' Organization 'should be open to all peace-loving states.' This proposal would be satisfactory ... if peace-lovingness were a permanent characteristic of most of them." (Richardson, 1960[a], p. 169.)

Perhaps war-mindedness is a permanent characteristic of most states. "During World War II," Richardson notes, "it was widely believed in Britain that Germans were the chief cause of war and that prevention of war simplified down to the prevention of German aggression.... But let us look at the facts.... They have been collected by a method especially designed to avoid bias for or against any people." (Richardson, 1960[a], p. 173.)

Some popular beliefs are challenged by Table 2 where national involvement, derived from the ratio of number of fatal quarrels in which the country was involved to number for the whole world, is shown for the period 1820 to 1945.

Table 2

NATIONAL INVOLVEMENT

Magnitude of fatal quarrel	7	6	5	4	4-7
Most involved nation	many equally	China	Turkey	Britain	Britain

A similar table prepared by Quincy Wright, by time period instead of by magnitude, names the most involved participants as: France (1550-1600); Spain (1600-1650); Britain (1650-1700); Britain (1700-1750); Russia (1750-1800); Britain (1800-1850); Britain (1850-1900); and for the whole time interval—Britain. (Richardson, 1960[a], p. 175.) Thus Britain actually had more wars than Germany over the period studied, despite what Englishmen thought during World War II.

Does this mean, as it seems to, that Great Britain

is the most aggressive, the most bloody-minded nation in recent centuries? Not really, for it is not that simple. In the first place, the data list involvement not aggression (since aggression is really very hard to define for nations) and in the second place, a number of variables are explicitly omitted from the analysis. One of the variables omitted is size of territory—an empire is much more likely to be involved in wars, one might surmise, than a country the size of Luxembourg; nor are the number of boundaries or frontiers considered.

Richardson found that when the number of frontiers which a nation (or empire) has in common with contiguous states is plotted against the number of foreign wars in which that nation (or empire) has been involved, an interesting correlation is revealed: "States have tended to become involved in wars in proportion to the number of states with which they have common frontiers." (Richardson, 1960[a], p. X, p. 297.) The correlation is in fact 0.77.

Nepal, for example, has two boundaries and has had three external wars during the period studied, while the French Empire with 15 frontiers has had 19 foreign wars. Only five nations are reported as having had no external wars; if civil wars are included, only one nation (Sweden) comes out with a clean bill of health: two boundaries, no wars of any kind.

In a typical Socratic dialogue, Richardson discusses the result:

> Federalist—Are we to understand that frontiers make wars, or that wars make frontiers? The diagram can be read either way.

> Author—Japan acquired frontiers with China and Russia as consequences of wars. Britain's numerous frontiers were certainly caused by colonization or conquest in earlier times. But between A.D. 1820 and 1939 the number of Britain's frontiers ... was successively 21, 24, 22, 23; that is almost constant. So expansion by conquest has not always increased the number of frontiers. Another and more thorough method for exploring the question is to notice whether states which had many wars were increasing the number of their frontiers, and vice versa. (Richardson, 1960[a], p. 181.)

Accordingly, Richardson separated the 33 nations which were included in his analysis into the 12 that had more than the average number of wars and the 21 that had fewer than the average number of wars. For each set the mean number of frontiers was computed at four dates: 1830, 1860, 1900, and 1929. Changes in the number of frontiers for both were found to be slight and irregular. One can therefore answer the federalist's question of cause and effect by concluding that for the period in question: Wars do not cause frontiers; rather, frontiers tend to cause wars.

COMMON GOVERNMENT AND WARS

It should be kept firmly in mind that Richardson's data indicate that frontiers do not cause war; they only tend to cause wars. In other words, there is a marked correlation between numbers of wars and numbers of different frontiers.

Of the 416 pairs of belligerents on Richardson's list of 305 wars (magnitude greater than 2.5), no fewer than 20 percent can be classed as civil wars. And in roughly one-third of these, the belligerents, rather than coming from two sections of the country, "have intermingled on the same territory up to the time when conflict began." In other words there were no boundary disputes. It is interesting to learn, however, that while half of the civil wars (or revolts) broke out after 23.5 years of common government, "the longer the groups have been united in common government, the less has been the probability of war between them." (Richardson, 1960a[a], p. xi.) Thus, common government must be considered a pacifying agent.

What about the effect of alliances? Richardson's results show that even after 25 years "there remains a general tendency for allies to group themselves as as before, although with many exceptions." (Richardson, 1960[a], p. 197.)

Common government and alliances are in a sense cooperative ventures. What about noncooperation or hostility? Among pairs of belligerents which previously had fought one another, Richardson asked, was revenge a motive? For exactly half of the combatants considered, he found that it was. Time would seem to be a useful healer, however, and the desire for revenge gradually receded as the time interval between wars increased. (Richardson, 1960[a], p. 197.) It would appear, therefore, as a general rule that the longer two groups of people have gone without war, the more likely it is that they will remain friendly.

ECONOMICS AND WARS

Of Richardson's 59 symbols, he assigned 11 of them to "economic causes of war." The validity of his assessment will be examined in Chapters 12 and 13, where all the evidence is subject to scrutiny. For the record, here is Richardson's complete economic compilation, with the exception of one or two items which have been shown together for convenience. Table 3 lists the number of occurrences of each "economic cause" for fatal quarrels from 1820 to 1929, of magnitude $4\frac{1}{2}$ to $7\frac{1}{2}$.

LANGUAGES AND WARS

Has common language had a beneficial effect on pairs of potential combatants? This question often has been asked, and with Richardson's data it can be answered statistically. When pairs of belligerents are itemized, it is found that approximately 200 pairs spoke different languages compared to 40 who shared a common tongue—ample confirmation, it would seem, of the theory that universal language would make the world a more peaceful place. Unhappily it is not that simple; before the case against Babel can be proven it is necessary to find out what would happen on the basis of straight probability. With wars taking place at random, more contestants will speak different languages than will speak the same language, for the world has a great many tongues. Richardson used for his analysis the 13 most common languages in the world as given in Whitaker's Almanac for 1941. Dialects have been subsumed under the name of the language of which they form a variety.

The calculation is complicated by whether one assumes that groups of people are likely only to go to war with their neighbours, or are equally likely to fight other groups anywhere in the world. While considering altercations between neighbours only would have made the calculations both easier and less ambiguous, Richardson, bearing in mind civil wars, chose to consider the interaction among all possible cells of people in the world, in which each cell had a population of at least one million persons. The same method of calculation was used in subsequent analyses of the effects of religion and of sovereignty on the probability of deadly quarrels. It may seem obvious that war between neighbouring groups of people is more probable than war between those remote from each other, but in view of the number of wars between imperialist nations and their colonies, or the confusions of World Wars I and II, such an assumption should be adopted with caution. Rather than making an arbitrary choice, Richardson made his computations on the basis of both approaches. The results are shown in Table 4, together with the population data on which they are based.

Using Table 4 as a reference it is impossible to reach firm conclusions regarding the pacifying effect of a common language for, with the exception of those cases which are underlined, the results are ambiguous. If model 1 is valid (equal chance of fighting anywhere), then not only is a common language not pacifying (with the single exception of Chinese), it

Table 3

NUMBER OF OCCURRENCES OF "ECONOMIC CAUSES" (Richardson, 1960[a], p. 209)

Economic causes of war given by historians	Magnitude of war 7	6	5	4	Total
Obstacles in the movement of trade				3	3
Commercial enterprises of one country in another			1	3	4
Restrictive immigration on part of one belligerent				3	3
Belligerents rivals in trading with third party	1		2	5	8
Individuals on the average richer in one state		1	3	7	11
One belligerent taxed by other			3	10	13
One belligerent wanted territory from other	1		5	27	33
TOTAL OCCURRENCES OF "ECONOMIC CAUSES"					75

Table 4

MAJOR WORLD LANGUAGES (Richardson, 1960[a], p. 223)

Language	Millions of speakers in 1801	1890	1940	Hypothetical pairs* of belligerents—same language (remote)	(neighbours)	Actual pairs* of belligerents—same language
Chinese			400	79	259	15 - 25
English	20	111	200	4	56	3 - 5
Russian	30	75	130	2	40	6 - 10
German	30	75	80	2	38	18 - 30
Spanish	26	42	75	1	23	42 - 96
Hindi			72	1	29	0 - 5
French	31	51	70	1	28	6 - 10
Japanese			70	1	22	3 - 5
Portuguese	7	13	50	0	6	3 - 5
Italian	15	33	50	0	17	3 - 5
Bengali			50	1	19	0
Malay			40	0	15	0
Arabic			40	0	15	3 - 19

* divided by total number of belligerent groups and times 1,000

appears to be an irritant; for the actual number of pairs of belligerents both speaking a given language was greater than the theoretical number of similar sized groups of people speaking a given language. But if model 2 is valid (only neighbours can fight) then a common language (with the single exception of Spanish) does reduce the likelihood of war, for the reverse is true: The theoretical number is greater than the actual number. Assuming the true model to lie somewhere between the two, we must conclude that similarities of language seem to have had little influence on the outbreak of war during the period studied.

RELIGION AND WARS

Richardson regards religion as ... "any firmly held belief about the world in general. Thus, after some hesitation, I have classed Marxist Communism as a religion, for it permeates the whole of life and is somewhat resistant to evidence. It has no god, but neither has Confucianism." (Richardson, 1960a, p. 233.) The key phrase to Richardson's definition is "firmly held," that is, resistant to change.

Do the world's various religions contribute to peace or to strife? The verdict of history seems to be—to strife. Many cases are recorded in which religion is cited as the cause of the war, while only two cases were found by Richardson during the course of his long study in which historians specifically mentioned religion as a pacifying influence. In 1810-24, Spanish America broke loose from Spain against the advice of the Pope, and in 1822 the Persians and Turks began peace negotiations partly because of their common Moslem faith. But these examples must be regarded as exceptions if one concedes the validity of Richardson's findings. When he treated the data statistically he concluded that religion tended to promote international belligerence. In all wars of magnitudes 3.5 to 7.5 between 1820 and 1929, there were 128 pairs of belligerents whose religion, broadly speaking, was the same, compared to 134 pairs with differences of religion. But, as with language, these figures must be compared to what would have happened on the basis of absolute chance. The results of this calculation are given in Table 5, together with the data upon which they are based.

Richardson neglected all but the top three religious groups, perhaps because of inadequate or insufficient data on conflicts between the other groups. As it is, however, no firm conclusions can be drawn concerning either Christianity or Mohammedanism when the belligerents are of the same faith. With the exception of the cases which are underlined, the results are ambiguous. Perhaps it is because the religion of the three groups of Christians, for example, is not really the same. But among the adherents of the religions of China there is a marked tendency towards pacifism. Is the effect one of language or religion or a third cause as yet unnamed? These figures do not tell us.

Using the same method of calculation, however, a second topic was examined by Richardson with a more definite result. Do belligerents with differences in religion fight more often than can be explained by pure chance? "There were more wars be-

Table 5

MAJOR WORLD RELIGIONS (Richardson, 1960[a], pp. 238-39)

Religion	Millions of adherents 1901	1934	Hypothetical pairs* of belligerents—same faith (remote)	(neighbours)	Actual pairs* of belligerents—same faith
Roman Catholics) Protestants) Greek and) Eastern Orthod.)	535	692	92	285	258 - 328
Mohammedans	180	209	16	113	22 - 42
Confucians Taoists and Buddhists		351	63	231	7 - 9
All others (Hindus, Jews, Animists, Shinto-ists & Marxists)	239	537			

* divided by total number of belligerent groups and times 1,000

tween Christians and Moslems," Richardson found, "than would be expected from their populations, if religious differences had not tended to instigate quarrels between them." (Richardson, 1960[a], p. 245.)

A study of national characteristics like religion, language or economic status is rewarding if these characteristics determine the likelihood of a nation's going to war. But what if there is no direct relationship between belligerency and national traits? What if warfare is a completely random affair, and any one country is no more or less likely to go to war than any other country? Or what if bellicosity is determined by geography, by the physical relationships between the various areas of the earth which we designate as nations?

On the surface, alliances and differences of religion, for example, seem to play a part in determining sets of belligerents. Are wars equally probable for all nations? At first glance, the answer again seems to be no; Sweden, for example, has avoided fighting for decades, while the Spanish-speaking nations frequently have been in trouble. Yet on the basis of straight probability, if warfare were a random business, there are bound to be great differences among nations which only a very large time interval would smooth out.

GEOGRAPHY AND WAR

What of geography? Are neighbouring countries at each other's throats more often than those far apart? And what of infectiousness? Do belligerents tend to "infect" the neutrals with the fever of war? We can answer these questions as long as we assume that we are not attempting to account for the actions of individual nations but only to determine the probability of a nation's going to war, given certain geographical circumstances.

The data for this statistical investigation by Richardson are the numbers of belligerents in his list of deadly quarrels, after the civil wars have been removed: 42 wars in which one group fought one other group, 24 wars in which one group fought two other groups, three wars in which two parties fought two others, and so on up to one war in which three fought four and another in which two fought five (War in La Plata, 1836-52, where the Blancos of Uruguay and Federalists of Argentina fought the Colorados of Uruguay, Unitarians from Argentina, the French, British and Brazilians). World Wars I and II were beyond the range of the table. Thirteen separate hypotheses are analyzed in Statistics of Deadly Quarrels, but only those which succeeded in explaining some of the historical facts are discussed here.

The first hypothesis, called localized quarrels (or chaos), accounts for all but the larger, more complicated wars. It states that disputes occur at random over the globe but that each dispute interests only a few nations; within this small group, the probability of war is the same for each pair of nations. In some ways, this first hypothesis is like the theory which explains the cohesion of molecules into minute clusters just before a gas turns into a liquid. Any molecule can start a cluster, but once started, the cluster attaches to itself a number of molecules from that immediate location.

Hypothesis two, called chaos restricted by geography, accounts for the larger, more complicated wars not handled by hypothesis one. It does so by treating the far-flung empires joined together by water separately from single, compact states. The hypothesis predicts and the historical facts confirm that the worldwide sea powers were much less pugnacious, considering the opportunities for conflict with other nations, than the land powers. Was distance from home base a factor as it was in Lorenz' animal studies? Richardson's statistics give us a clue but do not definitely answer the question.

The third hypothesis, chaos restricted by geography and modified by infectiousness, introduces one more idea: that the large wars are larger than they "should be"—a fact accounted for by the phenomenon of infectiousness: "Certainly infectiousness alone will not explain the facts; chaos alone is nearer the mark," Richardson states. "Only as a modifier of a geographically restricted chaos, can infectiousness be admitted into the theory." (Richardson, 1960a, p. 286.) What Richardson means is that wars would seem to be much more likely between contiguous states than between nations remote from each other. Where an empire is composed of separate spread-out geographical units, the likelihood of war is less than if the same-sized empire occupied one compact mass with borders shared by as many other nations. Also, once conflict begins, there is some tendency for it to spread out from the "infected" spot. But nations are not always unrelated units. In another chapter (Chapter 10) we will look at the effect of alliances.

NATIONALISM AND WARS

If the large wars are larger than they should be, to what is this due? Nationalism, perhaps? In search for some explanation of his results, Richardson turned his attention to another set of figures: the ratio between pairs of civil-war belligerents and pairs of foreign-war belligerents, a ratio which has some relation to geography. Richardson discovered that small wars more often are civil wars and larger wars more often are between different nations (see Table 6). This is not surprising, for in the extreme examples, murders (magnitude 0) all are civil, and "world wars" (magnitude 7) are nearly all international with only a small part of the overall conflict being civil war. And it is logical that the belligerents of the larger wars are generally of different nationalities since a larger theatre of operations is likely to include several countries.

But are civil wars smaller than they "should be"? Is a civil war in a country of 100 million, for example, smaller in extent than a foreign war between two countries each of 50 million? Does nationalism tend to restrict the size of civil strife or, alternatively, to enlarge foreign wars?

The figures of Table 6 were subjected by Richardson to calculations based on probability. He began by assuming that nationalism neither provokes foreign wars nor inhibits civilian strife, that it is all a matter of geography; but his calculations prove him wrong. Indeed, from the analysis, two important conclusions emerge: (1) "some strong pacifying influence has prevented small-scale fighting"; (2) "civil

Table 6

CIVIL AND FOREIGN WARS IN THE WORLD FROM 1820 to 1945
(Richardson, 1960[a], p. 297)

Magnitude of war		Pairs of belligerents (civil)	(foreign)	Ratio of civil pairs to total pairs
7		12	111	0.10
6		3	22	0.12
5		23	66	0.26
4		49	142	0.26
3	incomplete collection	129	153	0.46
2 and 1	unsystematic collection			
0	murders			1.00

fighting has been prevented more than foreign fighting." (Richardson, 1960a, p. 295.)

Why should this be so? Richardson cannot say, and he ends his book on a note of query:

> Though the existence of a pacifier is here proved, its nature is not entirely clear. It may well be the habit of obedience to a common government. But there are several other social features which have a positive correlation with common government...: intermarriage, common language, common religion, and the tendency to direct one's hatred on to foreigners ... no general pacifying effect was found for either common language or common religion ... " (Richardson, 1960a, p. 305.)

So we must look farther than Richardson for answers to the questions he himself raises.

SUMMARY

In summary, the following are some of the major conclusions from Statistics of Deadly Quarrels:

(a) States tend to become involved in war in proportion to the number of common borders they have with other states.

(b) When the total listing of various "economic causes" of war is compared to all other causes, they comprise 29 percent of the total.

(c) Of the various economic causes, "desire" for territory is the most frequent.

(d) The longer two groups of people have gone

without war, the more likely they are to remain at peace.

(e) Similarities of language and religion seem to have little pacifying effect.

(f) Differences of religion tend to cause war.

(g) War is more likely between neighbouring states than between states remote from each other.

(h) Common government (or some characteristic associated with common government like intermarriage or hatred of the foreigner) tends to inhibit the outbreak of civil war and to restrict its size, once started.

Richardson's conclusions are important, and remarkable in their extent, for they were compiled by hand calculations. Today an electronic computor could handle much of the work in minutes rather than months, and at the same time undertake more complex operations. The chief weakness of Richardson's conclusions, if one can even speak of weakness when referring to such a monumental contribution to the science of peace, is that they are univariate and not multivariate statistics. Thus, when two or more causes of war are involved, Richardson's methods are unable to disentangle the interactions between the several effects. For example, he could not say whether the Chinese language alone or the Chinese religion combined with the Chinese language has more of a pacifying effect. Multivariate analyses have been used by later investigators (see Chapters 7, 8, and 10), though Richardson's work has not been duplicated.

6 mathematical models

The scientific method can establish cause-and-effect relationships. These relationships may be biological (smoking is one of the causes of lung cancer), chemical (car engine exhausts are one of the causes of smog) or social (involving interactions between people). The most accurate way of expressing cause-and-effect relationships is through mathematical equations. Indeed, if the relationships are at all complicated—involving half a dozen variables, for example—then mathematics may be the only way of expressing the relationships; verbal expressions may no longer be adequate for prediction or even for description. The ideal in any scientific discipline is the elegance of mathematical expression which makes precise prediction possible.

Prediction may be only a statistical number (x number of people will die next year through automobile accidents) or a probability (there is a 60 percent probability of a thundershower in metropolitan Toronto tomorrow. On the other hand, prediction may be precise (there will be an eclipse of the moon at 21:05 Greenwich Mean Time on May 29, 1973). Reliable prediction is the goal of the scientific method, and ultimately the scientific method rests on mathematics. It is therefore desirable to place international relations, particularly as they involve conflict and war, on a mathematical basis. As a beginning step in this direction, Richardson has laid the groundwork for the application of mathematics to arms races.

ARMS AND INSECURITY

In Arms and Insecurity Richardson attempted to explain mathematically the dynamics of the war system and, especially, of arms races which, he hypothesized, were sometimes the cause of war. Richardson postulated that arms races follow an irrational course, a logic of their own. "What would occur," he asked, "if instinct and tradition were allowed to act uncontrolled?"

Richardson makes clear at the start that arms races only sometimes lead to war; historians explicitly mention them in only 10 of the 84 major wars which occurred from 1820 to 1929. Lest the historians had overlooked the obvious, however, Richardson and Carl Rosenberg looked into a sample of three of the 74 remaining wars (France versus the North German Confederation, 1868-70; Russia versus Turkey, 1872-77; and Russia versus Japan, 1901-04). Calculations of the military expenditures preceding these wars showed that arms races were slowing down, rather than accelerating, at the onset of war. (Richardson, 1960b, p. 71.) The warring nations' combined expenditures in the final year before the outbreak of war were less than in the previous year

Proof of a causal relation between arms races and war will, therefore, require more research. There is some purpose, nevertheless, in looking at arms races, per se, for the very process of interaction between belligerents may teach us something about war.

At the end of this book (Appendix) the two differential equations on which Richardson based his arms race theory are given. Since the symbolism of differential calculus will have little meaning for some readers, an algebraic translation of Richardson's reasoning appears below:

$$R = G + DY - FX \qquad (1)$$

where:

R is the rate at which the first side is increasing its armament expenditures.

G is the grievance or ambition of the first side towards the second side.

DY is the menace of the second side towards the first side;

Y is the annual armament expenditures of the second side, and

D is the defence coefficient of the first side.

FX represents the fatigue or expense of maintaining an arms race;

X is the annual armament expenditures of the first side, and

F is the fatigue coefficient of the first side.

Richardson assumed that the larger the armament expenditure, the less able a nation is to keep on increasing its military budget, so the last term in the equation (FX) is negative. G can be either positive, in which case it is truly grievance or ambition, or negative, in which case it represents the first side's good will towards the second side. If R represents the rate at which the second side is arming, the equation is the same, but the symbols' meanings are reversed (i.e. G is the grievance of the second side towards the first side).

The Richardson equations can tell us a great deal. Note that equation 1 includes time implicitly,* for R is the rate at which a belligerent is arming. Therefore, not only must the algebraic equation balance—the left-hand side of the equation always equals the right-hand side of the equation—but unless R is zero, the algebraic equation changes with time. A week or a year later, values of R, X and Y may be different, but the equation will still balance. As an example of this, let us assume that Side Two unilaterally disarms, that is, reduces its annual arms expenditures to zero. At that instant in time Y equals zero and Side One is no longer menaced. If Side One still has any ambition or grievance left, however, it will continue to arm until the fatigue of maintaining arms (FX) equals its ambition (G) when R becomes equal to zero. Thus, Side One stops increasing its arms expenditures (R = 0) but still maintains constant arms expenditures (X is positive). Since the armament expenditures of Side One are not zero (it has not disarmed), Side Two still is menaced and only if the good will of Side Two (which originally unilaterally disarmed) is sufficiently large (at least equal to the menace from Side One) will Side Two refrain from

* In the differential equations t is an explicit variable, as it is for the mathematical solution of the differential equation (see Appendix).

rearming. Thus unilateral disarmament relies on one side's maintaining good will in the face of the other side's ambition or grievance. Because such attitudes are unlikely to last, Richardson avers that unilateral disarmament is an impermanent state.

Next, consider mutual disarmament without satisfaction, that is, without good will on either side. For mutual disarmament, both X and Y must vanish, so R is equal to G. As long as G is positive, then the increase in arms expenditures of both sides will be positive or, in other words, rearmament will begin. Thus, mutual disarmament without satisfaction is always an impermanent state.

The effects of unilateral and bilateral disarmament can be readily deduced from the algebraic equation. Other conditions are not so obvious; but because the arms race has been expressed mathematically, they too can be determined mathematically.

The condition for "arms control" (that is, neither side increasing its arms but both maintaining a constant level of defence) is that the defence coefficient (D) be less than the fatigue coefficient (F). If D is greater than F, one of two things will happen: there will be a runaway arms race with expenditures increasing in an oscillating fashion or there will be a disarmament race with expenditures zigzagging down to zero (which can happen only if the G's are sufficiently negative—if there is enough good will on both sides).

The Richardson equations can and have been modified to account for additional assumptions. If rivalry not fear is the dominant passion, then the second term of the right-hand side of the equation becomes

D(Y-X) instead of DY. This means each side reacts to the difference between their two levels of military appropriations. Rivalry, it can be shown, automatically produces a condition of arms control in which an arms race is impossible, but disarmament can only occur if the grievance term G is zero. (Richardson, 1960[b], p. 36.)

But arms races have occurred—three of them in the 20th century—so it is fair to assert that fear rather than rivalry is at least sometimes the dominant passion.

WORLD WAR I

The arms race equations have been applied by Richardson to data for the period immediately preceding World War I (see Table 7). Individual defence budgets for four countries involved are listed for the years 1909 to 1913. Next the total annual expenditures of both sides are computed and shown for each year of this 5-year period; this corresponds to listing X + Y of the Richardson equations for each year of the period studied. Finally, annual increments of arms expenditures are shown; this corresponds to the sum for all countries of the left-hand term of the Richardson equations (R).

It can be readily deduced by simple addition of the two equations that a straight line will result if total annual increments are plotted against total annual expenditures.

thus for the first side

$$R_1 = G_1 + DY - FX$$

and for the second side

$R_2 = G_2 + DX - FY$

addition yields

$R_1 + R_2 = G_1 + G_2 + (D - F)(X + Y)$

where $X + Y$ is total annual expenditures

$R_1 + R_2$ is total annual increments

If $R_1 + R_2$ is plotted against $X + Y$ a straight line will result. The slope of the line is $D - F$, while the intercept of the line at the X-axis is minus $(G_1 + G_2)$ divided by $(D - F)$. When such a plot is made for World War I, $-(G_1 + G_2)/(D - F)$ turns out to be plus $970 million* and is therefore a measure not of grievance but of goodwill. (Richardson, 1960b, p. 33.) The slope of the line is plus 0.73; therefore D is greater than F. Thus, the international condition is not stable: it must either result in a runaway arms race or a race towards disarmament. Which? It all depends on the total value of $X + Y$.

Richardson's logic followed the course of his theory. An arms race was inevitable because by 1909 the total of $X + Y$ ($995 million) was already greater than the value of $-(G_1 + G_2)/(D - F)$ ($970 million). The explanation seems too easy; nevertheless, the simple theory fits well. There were greater difficulties with World War II.

* At an exchange rate of £1 = $5.00 (U.S.).

WORLD WAR II

When the arms race preceding World War II was plotted, a "dog-leg" appeared instead of a straight line, with the knee of the leg at 1933 (see Figure 2). Before 1933, the combined arms expenditures of both sides were increasing at a faster pace than afterwards (though Hitler came to power in 1933). The positive slope of both halves of the dog-leg, however, gave the same ominous verdict: an arms race was in progress. And though the slope after 1933 was less steep than before, in another way it was more serious, for G in the equation had changed from good will to grievance or, more aptly perhaps, to ambition. As Richardson said, "The word grievance suggests that nations strive only in gloom and depression to remedy intolerable wrong, whereas in fact they sometimes strive in pride and joy to extend an empire or enhance prestige." (Richardson, 1960[b], p. 229.) The reduced slope from 1933 to 1939 might suggest that the arms race was slowing down, but in fact it was steadily escalating. The reduced slope simply means that the two sides were *reacting* less to one another after 1933 than before, and were arming more out of grievance or ambition.

In an attempt to account for the shape of the curve or, rather, for the behaviour of the nations during the 1930's, Richardson modified his basic equations in a number of ways. Why did rearming suddenly start in 1929, 10 years after World War I, and what was the reason for the sudden shift in pace in 1933? Among Richardson's explanations were a fading of "war weariness," "submission of the defeated" and

Table 7

THE ARMS RACE OF 1909 - 1914 (Richardson, 1960[b], p. 32)
Defence budgets expressed in millions of $U.S.*

Country	1909	1910	1911	1912	1913
France	243	254	285	316	373
Russia	333	342	353	409	460
Germany	315	310	312	341	477
Austria-Hungary	104	117	123	127	134
TOTAL ANNUAL EXPENDITURES	996	1024	1074	1193	1445
TOTAL ANNUAL INCREMENTS		28	50.5	119	251.5

* on basis of £1 sterling equals $5 U.S.

Figure 2

THE ARMS RACE OF 1932 - 1939 (Richardson, 1960b, p. 242)

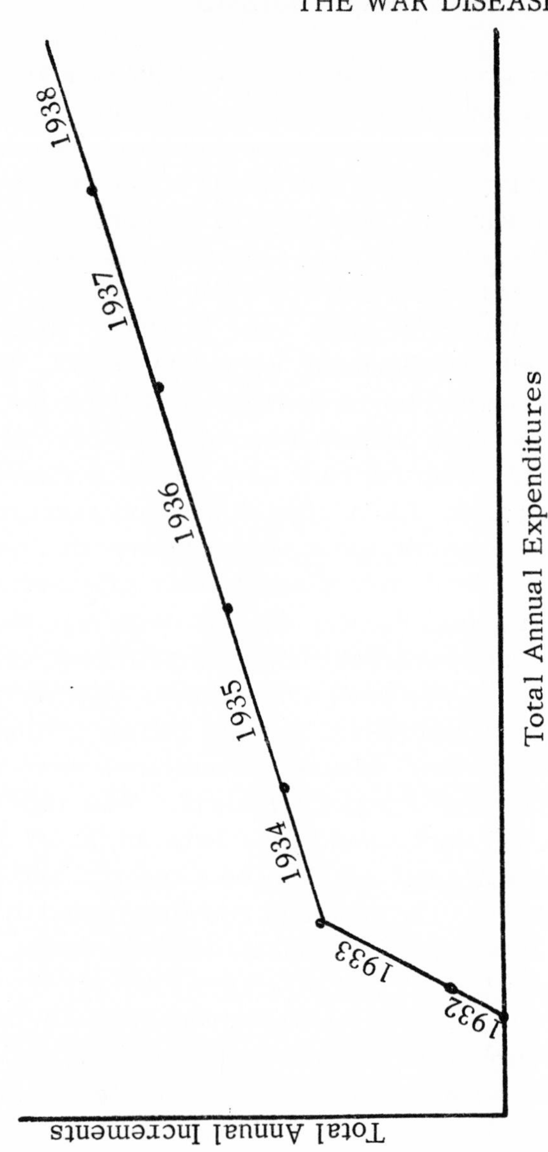

"the great trade depression." Hitler's ambitions were also suggested as worthy of study, but Richardson made no calculations for this latter hypothesis.

Submission—a depressing effect on the defence coefficient (D) caused by the overwhelming arms of the Allies at a time when Germany was nearly disarmed—accounts nicely for the 1919-33 period, including the renewal of the arms race in 1930. Richardson reasoned that Germany wanted to rearm, since in 1932 she applied to the League of Nations for permission to increase her armaments. The cost of armaments could not at that time have been a serious consideration; thus, FX of the Richardson equation must have been a small value. Moreover, the Germans had complained greatly about their grievances under the Versailles Treaty, so G certainly was positive. Therefore, for R to be near zero as it was from 1919 to 1929, the term DY must be negative. But Y was certainly positive, for the Allies had not disarmed; indeed their annual expenditures were many times that of the defeated Germans. Was this the clue? If the DY term could also have an X - Y factor in it, then that term could become negative and R could stay at zero. The resultant equation, found by Richardson to fit the historical facts, is of the form:

$$R = G + DY(1 + p(X - Y)) - FX \quad (2)$$

where p is the <u>submissiveness coefficient</u>.

Three effects could be accounted for by equation (2): the absence of German rearmament until 1929; its sudden appearance in 1929; and the actual arms race from 1929 to 1933, when $DY(1 + p(X - Y))$ was no no longer a negative term.

But submission could not account for the flattened

slope of the curve after 1933. Changes in the value of the arms-race coefficients themselves, D and F, seemed to be required for that. Mathematically it is easy to make the curve fit the facts, but how can it be justified? Was it altered German ambitions after the armistice (indicated by the return of war novels to popularity in Germany about 1927), or the effect of the world depression which hit Germany especially hard? Richardson's answer is that "all of these effects may have been operating together. I have not found any method for disentangling them." (Richardson, 1960[b], p. 260.)

WORLD WAR III

Paul Smoker attempted to fit Richardson's equations to the arms race which may be heralding World War III—the arms race of the present cold war. Three of the several models tested by Smoker will be considered here. In the first model, he compared the annual military expenditures of the United States with those of the Soviet Union for the years 1948 to 1960. (Smoker, 1964.) To account for inflation (or deflation), Smoker used the ratio of defence expenditures divided by total government budgets for his values of X and Y. Following Richardson's treatment of World War I, he plotted the sums of X and Y versus the annual increments of these sums in order to determine the total value of G for both sides and the value of D - F. The former value was slightly positive, indicating grievance or ambition rather than good will.

That the (D - F) factor was also positive confirmed that, according to the equations, an arms race was in progress. Or at least an arms race was in progress until 1952—as predicted by equation 1, the calculated points for the first 5 years fell nicely on a straight line, with a slope of 0.1. But in 1952, the slope turned abruptly downwards. Moreover, the line did not become a dog-leg as it had in the period preceding World War II, for several points were well off the upper half of the curve; points for the years 1955 and 1956 were especially errant. Significantly, these two dates follow hard on the heels of Germany's entry into NATO and Russia's signing of the Warsaw Pact.

Smoker's first study took no account of alliances. In his second study, therefore, he went well beyond a two-nation confrontation to a seven-nation world: the United States, Soviet Union, United Kingdom, China, West Germany, Poland and France. (Smoker, 1965.) By allowing for alliances, he expected that the 1955 and 1956 discrepancies would be explained. But Smoker went further: what if the reduced intensity of the arms race after 1952 was caused by some new and as yet unknown fear? Could Richardson's submissiveness equations still be made to fit the facts? In search of an answer Smoker applied his data to equation 2—without success. That the fit was better after 1952 was probably due to the study's extension to seven nations—but submission couldn't account for the abrupt change of slope any more than simple theory; nor could it satisfactorily account for the irregular points.

In the third model, Smoker explored an original

concept. (Smoker, 1966.) The calculations were made for the same seven nations used for model two but were based on equation 1; that is, the unsubmissive model. Before dividing the seven nations into two solid blocs, however, he worked out a polarization coefficient for each pair of countries, based on the ratio of trade between them compared to the total trade with all nations. In the extreme examples, two countries are either complete trading partners or have no trade at all. As one might expect, intermediate patterns generally exist; a nation (e.g., the United Kingdom) may trade more or less with nations from both sides of the cold war.

The polarization coefficient is +1 for a nation having no trade with nations of the other bloc, 0 for a nation trading equally with both blocs (hypothetically the coefficient would be -1 if all its trade were with nations of the opposing bloc). Values used by Smoker fell in the range from 0 to +1.

Assuming that trade is a measure of relaxed tensions, Smoker has used the polarization coefficient as a multiplier of the defence expenditures for individual nations in each bloc of the East-West confrontation. He thus has been able to analyze the arms race for the whole period from 1948 to 1962 and to obtain a remarkable fit with one exception: the dog-leg was still there with its knee at 1952. Even to obtain so good a fit, it had been necessary to use two different values for the term D - F. In other words, around 1952 a new element of fear (or perhaps a new awareness of costs) was introduced into the world because, from 1952 to 1962, the arms race deescalated slightly. What caused the fear or the new awareness? The

H-bomb, perhaps. It seems reasonable to assume that with a thousandfold "bigger-bang-for-a-buck," defence expenditures would start to level off.

The entry of West Germany into NATO in 1954 and the formation of the Warsaw Pact in 1955 caused only slight irregularities in the curve of model three and did not affect its general trend.

INSTANTANEOUS AGGRESSIVE ACTION

A slightly different interpretation of the Richardson equations is given by Robert Abelson. (Abelson, 1963.) In place of cumulative armaments, he has used "instantaneous aggressive actions"; for "defence" and "fatigue" coefficients he has used "sensitivity" and "forgiveness" coefficients. In Richardson's system the acquisition of armaments represents a semi-permanent aggressive commitment, while in Abelson's system the instantaneous aggressive actions are of short-term duration. It is assumed that the actions of each group represent a provocation for the other, which will respond in kind.

Abelson's formulation is in part based on a remark by the sociologist David Reisman: "Each crisis, like fall-out, produces cumulative poisons with a long half-life in American domestic politics." It might also have been based on the conclusion reached as a result of Richardson's work (see page 54) "the longer two groups of people have gone without war, the more likely it is that they will remain friendly." Each says the same thing with a different emphasis: that belligerent acts have a long-term effect but that, over time, the effect decreases. Abelson concludes that, "if either group is interested in avoiding a provocative spiral, it might do so by responding with moderation to the other's provocations, or by forgiving them rapidly, or both," which in Richardson's language is equivalent to saying, "an arms race can be avoided by a reluctance to increase armaments in response to an increase by the other side (low D), or by a greater concern for the cost of the armaments (high F), or both."

The greater versatility of interpretation is attractive; as Abelson says, "since the two interpretations lead to identical mathematical results, the generality of the Richardson model is strengthened." (Abelson, 1963.) The Richardson arms race equations describe preparations for war; they do not describe war itself. Alcock and Lowe (1969), however, considered that a war itself might follow an action-and-reaction process; specifically they hypothesized that the Vietnam war might be described by the Richardson arms race equations. Annual casualty figures for all major belligerents (United States, South Vietnam, N. L. F. and North Vietnam) were recorded for the period 1962 to 1968. Differences in total annual casualties between successive pairs of years were plotted versus the mean of total annual casualties for successive pairs of years for the period 1962 to 1968. The result was a dog-leg curve similar to that for the arms race preceding World War II, with the knee of the dog-leg at December 1964.

In a search for causation, the investigators compiled a list of over 300 events connected with the Vietnam war over the period studied. An inspection of the most significant of these events lead them to conclude that the Tonkin Bay incident in August 1964 and subsequent U.S. Senate resolution was crucial in accounting for the sharp change in battle casualties. They summarized: "Since one of the key variables is the attitude of the leaders, and since the men in Washington were given a strong new mandate from the American people in November 1964, this may be the explanation of the change in slope in early 1965."

Other scholars have employed battle casualties as primary data for investigating the dynamics of war itself. John Voevodsky (1969), for example, has made a comparative analysis of five wars: the American Civil War, World Wars I and II, Korea, and Vietnam. With the exception of the break point in December 1964 (his work therefore confirms the study by Alcock and Lowe) which causes Voevodsky to regard Vietnam as two wars, he concludes that "the repetitive behavioral patterns of nations at war, particularly the United States, our allies, and our enemies during the last 100 years, reveals that we and the enemy are acting today in the same way as we have acted in the past."

What is that "repetitive behavioral pattern?" Voevodsky assumes that all living systems are characterized by feedback-controls which can be described by linear second-order differential equations* of the sort used by Lewis Richardson for his arms equations. The solutions to these equations are exponential in nature. Indeed, if one is not concerned

* A linear second-order differential equation for a mechanical system includes a term for acceleration, whereas a linear first-order equation is limited to velocity.

with the early stages of the war, first-order differential equations appear to describe accurately the time-variant nature of the vital statistics. Two parameters of Voevodsky's first-order war equation uniquely describe any specific war: a characteristic time constant (how long the war will last), and a theoretical maximum strength (how many men ultimately will die in the war). Thus, if the time of fighting is divided by the characteristic time constant for any given war, and if the total number of deaths at any given time is divided by the theoretical maximum strength for the given war, battle deaths for all five wars studied by Voevodsky can be described by a single mathematical equation and battle deaths versus time can be plotted with a single line. Once again, the generality of the Richardson model seems to have been strengthened.

Apparently the arms expenditures of a nation may be predictable as a result of interaction between two belligerents; moreover, following the onset of war, battle casualties may be predictable as a result of the interaction between two belligerents. Forecasts of this nature, therefore, must be regarded as preliminary evidence for Richardson's premise that people act automatically, or as "if they did not stop to think." (Richardson, 1960b, p. 12.)

7 sociological evidence---beliefs

One of this book's basic assumptions is that research can make an important contribution to the solution of the problem of war and peace, particularly in those fields which are amenable to objective measurement.

"One of these fields," note the pyschologist John Paul and the sociologist Jerome Laulicht, "is the study of public opinion." As they point out:

> While public opinion may be well-informed or ill-informed, constant or fleeting, wise or stupid, what it is at any given time is a measurable fact. Further, it is a fact which has both practical and scientific implications.
>
> The practical implications are in terms of the actual impact of accurate assessment of public opinion on foreign policy. In a democracy public opinion can, at times, initiate new measures, but more frequently it acts as a limiting factor on government policy. Democratic governments have periodically to face the electorate and, to the extent that they want to get re-elected, they

> tend to undertake policies which they believe to be popular with, or at least acceptable to, the majority of the electorate. This does not mean that governments should or do base their policies exclusively on public opinion. They are also expected to provide leadership and to rule with the consent of the governed. This means in effect that if a democratic government wishes to pursue a policy which is not popular it has to undertake a major effort to explain its reasons to the voters in the hope that the policy will become popular or at least acceptable. (Paul and Laulicht, 1963, p. 1.)

The scientific implications of a public opinion study come from analyses of the data. Thousands of bits of information are normally recorded, and the very volume of this information lends itself to the kinds of analysis made possible by computers. Correlations can be made between the various attitudes held and between the attitudes and other characteristics of the people interviewed.

CANADIAN ATTITUDES

A comprehensive single-nation study of attitudes towards war and peace was carried out during 1962-64 by the Canadian Peace Research Institute. (Paul and Laulicht, 1963.) In late 1962, personal interviews were conducted with a representative sample of 1,000 Canadian citizens of voting age and, in early 1963, with three elite groups which consisted of 48 leading businessmen, 48 trade union leaders and 48 political leaders. The national sample was drawn, on an area basis, from all towns and cities with a population of more than 1,000 and from 72 selected districts in the country to cover the rural population. Because they were difficult to canvass, the northern half of Newfoundland, and all of the Northwest Territories were excluded.

The random sample of businessmen was selected from Canadian residents who were either members of the board of directors of one of Canada's 10 chartered banks or presidents of companies with assets exceeding $100 million.

The random sample of union leaders was selected from Canadian residents who were either senior officers of national trade union federations or leaders of national unions with memberships exceeding 10,000.

The political leaders were chosen in proportion to party standings in the House of Commons at the time of the survey. Eighteen of them were cabinet ministers or members of opposition "shadow" cabinets; five were senior advisers to cabinet ministers; the remaining 25 were members of Parliament, 20 of whom were members of the Foreign Affairs Committee or delegates to NATO or to the United Nations.

The survey was conducted by structured interviews, and the questionnaire used had been gradually amended to eliminate ambiguous, overlapping and too difficult items. (The 11th version was the one finally accepted.) The first two pages of the four-part interview contained questions about the respondent and about topics which were found to be good rapport-builders. For instance, a question about the national health plan was asked first; most people had opinions about it and were happy to express them. (All questions about peace and war had to be eliminated from the first two pages in order to reduce the refusal rate.) Then there were questions seeking opinions about foreign and defence policy, followed by questions to test factual knowledge about foreign affairs and defence policy. The last three pages dealt with biographical information.

Question 9, for example, asked:

"Canada spends about 54 million dollars a year on foreign aid—that is helping underdeveloped countries (for example, the Colombo plan). How do you feel about this?

"(a) Is it too much, too little, or about right?

"(b) Should this money be given through the U.N., or directly by one country to another?

"(c) If both ways; should most of the money be given through the U.N., mostly given directly, or should about half of it be given through the U.N. and half directly?"

Question 12, also a multiple-choice question, asked:

"Which of these statements comes closest to the way you feel about whether a person can or should do anything to prevent war?

"(a) I think nothing anyone can do will stop atomic war.

"(b) There is nothing I have to do because really there is little danger of an atomic war.

"(c) There is nothing I can do. It is the government's responsibility since they have the power and information.

"(d) People should become involved in efforts to prevent war; but I don't have the time or money to do anything myself.

"(e) It is my duty to find out what I can do personally, and do it even if it costs me time and money."

A typical knowledge question is number 46:

"About how big is the U.N. budget?

"(a) It is about the same or smaller than the amount New York City spends on police and fire protection.

"(b) It is smaller than the Canadian budget, but bigger than the Ontario budget.

"(c) It is about the same as the Canadian budget.

"(d) It is smaller than the American budget, but larger than that of Canada."

(a) is correct, of course, or was in 1962 when the regular United Nations budget was slightly more than 80 million dollars. Even if one added to it the cost of the U.N. emergency forces during the Congo crisis and other additional expenses which are not part of the regular budget (e.g., the Technical Assistance Program or the Children's Fund), it did not exceed $400 million per year. The budget for New York City police and fire protection in 1962 was $385 million.

Examples of questions designed to elicit significant biographical data, in addition to those about age and sex, are: "What is your religious denomination? About how often do you attend church (or temple)? "Has any member of your immediate family been badly wounded as a direct result of war, or died as a direct result of war?"

Two kinds of results were obtained from the survey: statistical tabulations of the responses from all groups and a thorough analysis of the data. The tabulations are interesting and useful. For example,

Table 8 shows the answers to question 9a for the various groups tested.

Can a person, or should he, do anything to prevent war? Some 34 percent of the general public thought that it was their duty to find out what they could do personally even if it cost them time and money. About 58 percent of the leading businessmen, 87 percent of labour leaders and 90 percent of the political leaders agreed.

In the knowledge questions, the businessmen and politicians both scored 25 percent in assessing the size of the U.N. budget (this could have been reached by pure chance since there were four choices). Most members of all groups overestimated the U.N. budget, and 24 percent of the general public even thought that it was larger than that of Canada (in 1962 about $17 billion).

The second set of results from the attitude survey—the computer analyses—are immensely more valuable for our purpose (understanding the causes of war) than are the first "raw" data. Three types of analyses have been found useful, and since some of the same techniques will be referred to later in this chapter they should be described briefly: (Laulicht and Strong, 1967.)

Guttman scaling consists of grouping questions about the same topic (say foreign aid or the U.N.) to form a single measure of the attitude in question (a scale perhaps of from 1 to 5). It is a basic law of opinion-testing that, though single questions are seldom reliable, clusters of questions are more meaningful. The clusters can be arranged into scales which indicate the intensity of feeling of the attitude

Table 8

RESPONSES TO FOREIGN AID QUESTION FROM GROUPS TESTED

Canada spends about $54 million dollars a year on foreign aid.

Is it:

Response	National sample	Businessmen	Labour leaders	Politicians
Too much	23%	4%	2%	6%
About right	51	21	13	21
Too little	12	44	75	73
No aid should be given	3	0	0	0
Don't know or no opinion	11	31	10	0

held, just as shades of colour can be arranged on a scale, from the lightest blue to the deepest indigo. The Guttman scale is simply a technique for seeing that certain questions can be brought together.

Factor analysis (mentioned in Chapter 3) is a mathematical simplifying technique which clusters scales together into factors, just as Guttman scaling groups individual items together to form scales. Scales within a given factor "correlate" with one another; they also "load" on the factor. Scales can load on more than one factor, but the higher the loading the less likely this is to occur.

A multiple regression analysis also compares the various scales, not by clustering variables into a number of independent unnamed "factors," but by determining the relationship between the known scales directly. Thus, all variables but one are specified as independent variables, while one becomes the dependent variable whose value is predicted by the value of the various independent variables. The more the dependent variable is really related to, or dependent on, the independent variables, the more its value can be predicted by them. Each variable in turn can be treated as dependent to find out to what extent it correlates with the others.

The opinion survey produced 12 significant scales, nine measuring attitude, one measuring knowledge and two giving important biographical characteristics. Because subsequently seven of the 12 variables were used as independent variables to predict the values of the remaining five dependent variables, we have listed them under both categories. The choice, in part arbitrary, is intended to suggest a cause-and-effect relationship. Level of education is not the result of attitude towards the U. N., for example; the reverse is more likely to be true.

Dependent variables are attitude towards:

(a) Strengthening the United Nations and related international institutions.

(c) Canadian acquisition of nuclear weapons and their spread to nations which do not yet have them.

(d) The arms race and the size of Canadian defence forces, with emphasis on conventional forces.

(e) Negotiations about disarmament, trade and co-existence with Communist countries, partially a measure of trust.

Independent variables, or predictors, are:

(f) Level of formal education.

(g) Level of knowledge about foreign policy.

(h) Religious affiliation and level of church attendance. The scale called religious dogmatism is based on the extent of dogmatic beliefs essential to the faith (Roman Catholics, Baptists and Presbyterians are high on this scale; atheists, agnostics, Quakers, and Unitarians are low; United Church, Anglicans and Lutherans come in between).

(i) Attitude towards the sense of responsibility which the average person and various groups (scientists, churches, labour and businessmen) should have in efforts to prevent war.

(j) Attitude towards social welfare and the expansion of government welfare programs and government activities designed to stimulate the economy.

(k) Attitude of cynicism with regard to whether Russians and Americans, both leaders and people, have a desire and readiness for general disarmament now.

Among the variables tested which seem to have little or no relationship to defence and foreign policy attitudes are: age; sex; military experience or personal suffering as a result of war; place of residence (city, town or country); social class, occupation or income; ethnic origin; and concern over the possible serious economic consequences of disarmament. Since this last item is of particular interest, it was tested both as an independent and dependent variable and included in innumerable factor analyses. The result was entirely negative—it does not relate to any of the other variables.

The various multiple regression equations were determined by lumping together the results for the three elite groups, plus the English-speaking portion of the national sample, and running regression analyses on this composite sample. Since the French-speaking portion of the national sample (respondents) was not included in this calculation, the predictive accuracy of the final equations could be tested by calculating values for the five dependent attitudes from numerical values for the six independent variables and comparing the calculated values with the actual measured values for the French-Canadian sample (See Figure 3—conventional forces is omitted since it was based on only one independent variable).

Results of the CPRI attitude study indicate that the three elite groups—business, labour and political—

have much less desire than the general public for nuclear weapons or conventional forces and more desire for coexistence with Communist nations, with one exception: Business leaders favour conventional forces and nuclear weapons and oppose strengthening the United Nations more than any other group (see page 99). (Laulicht, 1965c.)

Concern over the economic consequences of disarmament is not linked in any way to the other variables. This suggests that if fear of disarmament exists it is not a deeply rooted attitude for any of the groups measured. Respondents did, however, think that others would be concerned.

In general, correlations between the variables are low (.35 to .75), so prediction of individual attitudes is impossible. But prediction of group foreign policy attitudes (e.g., French-Canadian) on the basis of group characteristics is remarkably accurate.

Level of education, sense of social responsibility and a positive attitude towards social welfare are the most powerful predictors of "international attitudes"; that is, a desire to strengthen the United Nations and to give more foreign aid.

Level of education (and knowledge), positive attitude towards social welfare and absence of religious dogmatism are the most important predictors of peaceful attitudes; that is, a desire for coexistence and little desire for nuclear weapons and conventional forces.

In the factor analyses of the national sample and all three elite groups, two factors consistently emerged. (Laulicht, 1965a.) The first factor linked attitudes towards coexistence and both nuclear and convention-

Figure 3

MEASURED VALUES OF WAR/PEACE ATTITUDES FOR FIVE CANADIAN GROUPS

(Businessmen, Labour Leaders, Politicians, English and French Canadians)

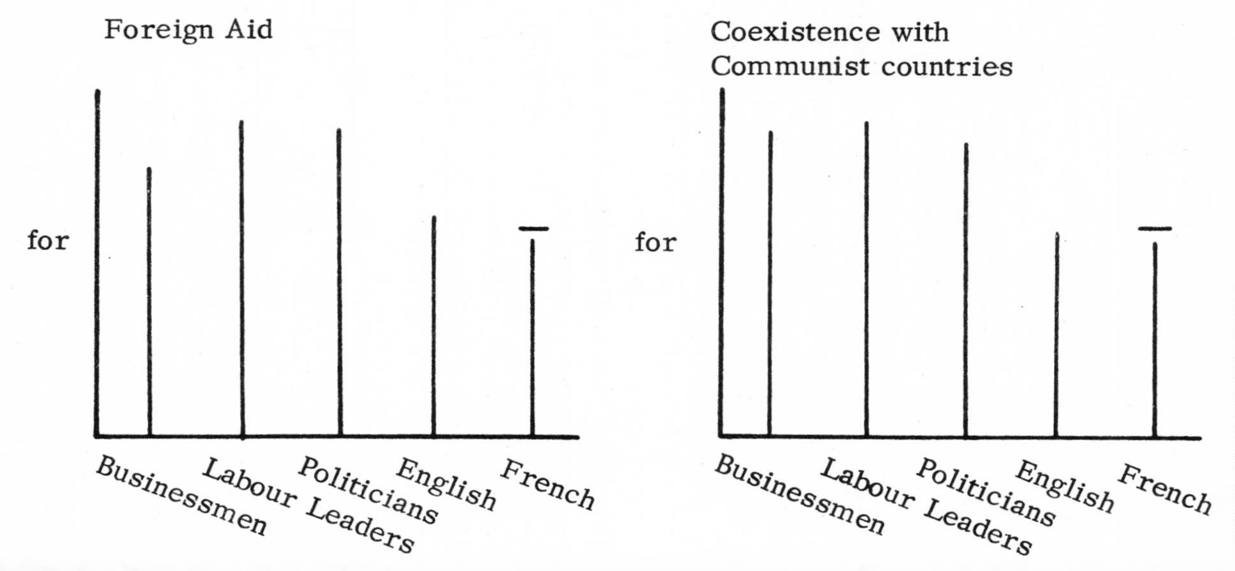

Figure 3 (continued)

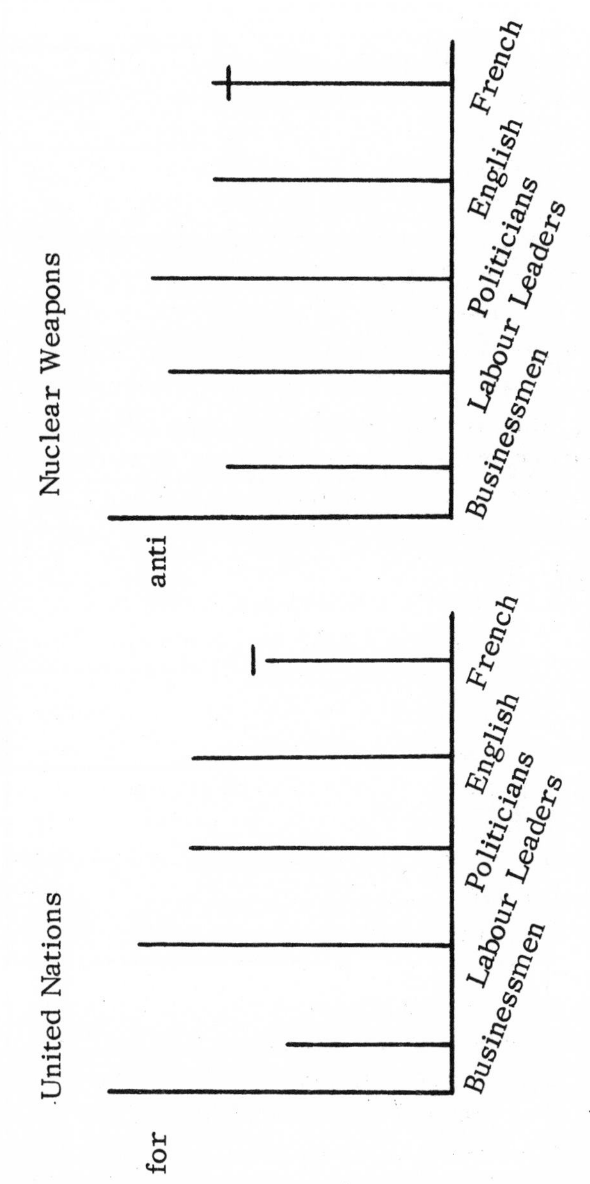

The crossbars of the French Canadian sample are calculated values based on six other variables.

al weapons with cynicism and religious dogmatism. The findings indicated that the more cynical and the more dogmatic people were more in favour of nuclear and conventional weapons and less in favour of coexistence. A second factor, in general, linked positive attitudes towards the United Nations and foreign aid with high scores of responsibility, social welfare, knowledge and/or education. To explore these relationships further, multiple regression analyses were made for all dependent variables. The results are shown in Table 9. All independent variables which help to account for the values of the various dependent variables are indicated with an X, though in practice an actual equation in deduced. Thus, the equation expressing attitude towards the giving of foreign aid is:

foreign aid = 1.72 + 0.22 responsibility + 0.21 knowledge + 0.15 education + .05 social welfare

The CPRI opinion survey was conducted among Canadians, for whom the "enemy" is international Communism. Ideologically, Canadians are committed to democracy, Christianity and the capitalist system. The Canadian, then, sees the enemy as totalitarian, atheistic and socialistic; and not surprisingly, those Canadians who are most antithetical to these values are most war-like in their attitudes.

The survey found that level of education for all groups tested is a consistent predictor of peaceful and international attitudes, but age, sex, income, social class, place of residence (urban or rural), and military experience had little or little or no effect on defence and foreign policy attitudes.

Table 9

MULTIPLE REGRESSION ANALYSIS OF BUSINESSMEN, LABOUR LEADERS, POLITICIANS AND ENGLISH-SPEAKING CANADIANS (Laulicht, 1965[b])

Dependent Variables	Independent Variables					
	Education	Knowledge	Religious Dogmatism	Responsibility	Social Welfare	Cynicism
United Nations	X	X		X	X	
Foreign Aid	X	X		X	X	
Nuclear Weapons	X		X	X	X	
Conventional Forces			X			
Coexistence	X	X	X		X	X

AMERICAN ATTITUDES

An opinion survey cannot reveal attitudes not incorporated in its questions. Thus, for example, the Canadian attitude study reveals no correlations between nationalism or authoritarianism and war-like beliefs, for the simple reason that questions on nationalism or authoritarianism were not included in the questionnaire. There is one study, however, that does shed light on this question, as well as providing valuable corroboration for several of the CPRI findings. (Eckhardt, et al., 1967.)

Psychologist William Eckhardt and his colleagues in the Des Moines Peace Research Group administered a questionnaire which included a 14-item "Militarism" Scale to over 2,000 American subjects during the years 1962-64. Subjects included groups of college students, junior and senior high school students, reserve officers and ROTC students, pacifist adult and student groups, unspecified adult groups and 10 groups of mental patients.

While higher-than-average militarism scores were obtained for the reserve officers and ROTC students and lower-than-average scores were found for the pacifist groups, there was no significant difference in militarism scores between the other groups of subjects, including the mental patients.

Eckhardt's questionnaire included items designed to measure attitude towards capitalism, conservatism, communism, welfarism, nationalism, patriotism, democracy and authoritarianism of the right. His study also included scales of religious orthodoxy and materialism versus intellectualism. Simple correlations of all these variables with the Militarism Scale were then obtained, with the following results:

The Militarism Scale was found positively correlated with the capitalism and conservatism scales, negatively with the communism and welfarism items. "These results would suggest," the researchers report, "that approximately 25 percent of the variance (see Glossary) in Militarism scores could be explained by favourable attitudes towards capitalism and/or adverse attitudes towards socialism."

The Militarism Scale also was found to be correlated negatively with attitude toward democracy and correlated positively with religious orthodoxy, nationalism, patriotism and anti-intellectualism. Authoritarianism of the right correlated positively with one of the four factors making up the Militarism Scale. Summing up his work, Eckhardt says that much of the variance of the militarism scores may be explained by the following five variables: capitalism, authoritarianism, nationalism, materialism (anti-intellectualism) and religious orthodoxy.

Not only are there no major contradictions between the American and Canadian attitude studies, there is a startling similarity. The CPRI Militarism Scale could be said to have consisted of three major factors: support for nuclear weapons, distrust of communism and reliance on conventional force. The Eckhardt Militarism Scale consisted of four factors, three of which are of major importance: belief in military deterrence, presumably nuclear (six items of the questionnaire); distrust of communist nations (three items), and belief that government leaders wanted to disarm (three items). The CPRI Militarism Scale was dependent on level of education (negatively), religious dogmatism and attitude towards social welfare (negatively), while the corresponding Eckhardt scale was dependent on anti-intellectualism, religious orthodoxy, authoritarianism, attitude towards capitalism and nationalism.

ELITE ATTITUDES

A questionnaire is one way of assessing the attitudes of people and of special groups of people (elites). The attitudes of leaders of major powers, however, are more elusive, usually because it is difficult to gain access to them sufficiently often, if at all. Therefore another method has been developed in recent years which allows scientific analysis of a leader's views without a personal interview. The method (called content analysis) provides a systematic profile of the content of his speeches, based on a certain number of key words which are indicative of his feelings towards certain topics and of the strength of those feelings. Content analysis is concerned with the leader's "image" of the situation rather than with "objective" reality, for as Ole Holsti explains: "decision makers act upon their definition of the situation and their images of states—others as well as their own. These images are in turn dependent upon the decision maker's belief system, and these may or may not be accurate representations of 'reality.' Thus it has been suggested that international conflict frequently is not between states, but rather between distorted images of states." (Holsti, 1962.)

To explore this relationship between belief system

and national image, Holsti examined all the public statements made by John Foster Dulles concerning the Soviet Union during the 1953-59 period. There were 434 documents including Congressional testimony, press conferences and addresses. All of Dulles' statements concerning the Soviet Union were translated into 3,584 "evaluative assertions" and placed into one of four categories:

(1) Soviet policy: assessed on a friendship-hostility continuum (2,246 statements).
(2) Soviet capabilities: assessed on a strength-weakness continuum (732 statements).
(3) Soviet success: assessed on a satisfaction-frustration continuum (290 statements).
(4) General evaluation of the Soviet Union: assessed on a good-bad continuum (316 statements).

When all four variables are plotted against time over the 1953-59 period, the top three rise and fall together; that is, in the first quarter of 1954, Soviet hostility, capability and success, as seen by Dulles (his attitude towards, or image of, the Soviet Union), are all peaked, while all three fall to a minimum plateau in 1955-56, then rise to a maximum in 1958.

Dulles' personal beliefs (the independent or predictor variable) were those of an American Puritan, so his image of the Soviet Union (the dependent or predicted variable) was assumed to be built on the trinity of atheism, totalitarianism and communism—a negation of the values at the core of his personal belief system. Thus, hypothesized Holsti, all information concerning the Soviet Union would tend to be perceived and interpreted in a manner consistent with Dulles' belief system: Soviet hostility or friendliness towards the United States (the first variable of the analysis), would not go up and down as the country changed for the better or worse (the fourth variable of the analysis), but solely because their capability had increased or decreased, or because they had previously experienced success or failure in their foreign policy. This is exactly what the content analysis showed; although hostility matched the rise and fall of Soviet capability and success over the period, Dulles' good or bad evaluation (variable four) showed no change, up or down. To Dulles, the enemy was bad by definition and all knowledge he acquired had to be distorted to conform to his image. It is an excellent example of what Milton Rokeach calls "the closed mind." (Rokeach, 1960.)

Perception of hostility may cause a leader to respond in a hostile manner. To test for a possible relationship between the perception of an enemy state's hostility and a hostile decision by one's own government leaders, Professor Dina Zinnes used the content analysis technique. (Zinnes, 1962.) As an illustration, two decisions made during the 6-week crisis prior to the outbreak of war in 1914 were selected for analysis. The period of time preceding each decision was used as the unit of time for the study (so that a cause-and-effect relationship could be assumed) and the written diplomatic communications sent out by the decision-making state during the period were subjected to analysis. The two events were the Austrian decision to send an ultimatum to Serbia on July 19 and the Russian decision to mobilize her entire armed forces on July 30. Zinnes relates:

Though greatly simplified, the following description represents the generally accepted interpretations of these events. Difficulties had existed between Serbia and Austria-Hungary for a number of years due in part to territorial disagreements; certain elements in Serbia had aspirations for a "Greater Serbia" which would inevitably involve land held by Austria. Then on June 28, 1914 the Archduke Franz Ferdinand, heir to the Austrian throne, was assassinated in Sarajevo, the capital of Bosnia. Bosnia was one of the disputed areas, and Austria drew the obvious conclusion, although proof of Serbian complicity in the crime was only to be discovered considerably later.... By July 19 the final decision had been made and implemented: Austria would present Serbia with an ultimatum so severe as to almost require its rejection by a sovereign power. And Austria would make it clear that rejection meant war...." (Zinnes, 1962.)

A number of hypotheses were tested. We will consider, for the sake of brevity, only those of significance:

(a) The more often X sees himself as the object of hostility, the more states he sees as being hostile towards him. (The correlation was 0.95.)

(b) The more hostile statements X makes, the more hostility he will perceive in the environment. (The correlation was 0.93.)

Thus, perception of others' hostility is significantly correlated with one's own emission of hostility, and the data suggest that for these historical events, emotion was an important factor. At the beginning of her report, Zinnes wrote:

> Decision-making studies have generally been concerned with the "rationality" of the decision process. Only by implication and assumption is there a treatment of the emotional factors in the decision mechanism. The purpose of this paper is to raise the question of the relationship of emotion to decision-making and to attempt the beginnings of a partial answer.

The partial answer turned out to be affirmative, for emotion has been definitely shown to play an important part in decision-making.

8 psychological evidence---personality

The four studies reviewed in the previous chapter dealt mainly with beliefs held by various individuals, e.g., their ideological views about militarism, nationalism, democracy, capitalism or the United Nations. Since neither an individual's personality nor his early training were considered, such studies do not, of course, uncover the causes of the particular values held. To this end, however, many other investigators have looked into the relationships between ideology and personality and between personality and childhood training.

WAR/PEACE ATTITUDES AND PERSONALITY

In 1967-68, William Eckhardt administered a 470-item questionnaire to 122 Canadian subjects, aged 14-61, who were equally divided among adults and students and men and women. Average age was 29, and average education was almost 14 years. The 470 items were obtained from 71 psychological scales whose reliabilities and validities had already been established. (Eckhardt and Lentz, 1967.) They included the authoritarian personality scales, the Minnesota Multiphasic Personality Inventory scales, several neuroticism and extraversion scales, several childhood discipline scales and a number of militarism, nationalism and conservatism scales. (Adorno et al., 1950; Dahlstrom and Welsh, 1960; Eysenck, 1959; Comrey and Newmeyer, 1965; for example.) In other words, a wide variety of previously researched ideological and personality scales were included in this questionnaire, along with several demographic variables: sex, education and political and religious preference. Subjects were instructed to rate each item from one to five according to whether they strongly or mildly disagreed, were neutral about the question or mildly or strongly agreed.

When the scores of the 122 subjects on 71 scales were correlated with each other and factor analyzed, the 71 scales became grouped into 18 "primary factors," of which seven were mainly ideological factors and therefore were relatively free of personality scales, and 11 were personality factors which were relatively free of ideological scales. (Eckhardt and Alcock, 1970.) The first two ideological factors (militarism and religiosity) and the first two personality factors (neuroticism and extraversion) duplicated the results of many other studies conducted during the past 30 years or more. The next two ideological factors (conservatism and nationalism) and the next two personality factors (misanthropy and childhood discipline as recalled by the subject) also had been isolated by previous investigators. But including items touching on all of these factors into a single questionnaire was a new approach. The most highly weighted of the 18 primary factors are given in Table 10, together with the various scales making up each factor.

"Ideology and personality were relatively independent of each other at the primary level of analysis," Eckhardt writes; "however, inspection of scales and items suggested that the major ideological and personality factors all contained a common quality which was called "compulsion" to signify a readiness to use force or the threat of force, punishment or the threat of punishment, as a means of controlling human behavior and of resolving conflict situations, whether these situations were intrapersonal (as in neurosis), interpersonal (as in extraversion and misanthropy), intranational (as in conservatism), international (as in militarism and nationalism), or spiritual (as in religiosity)." (Eckhardt and Alcock, 1970, p. 107.)

Consequently, calculations were made of the correlations between the 18 primary factor scores; these factors were further analyzed and then grouped into five "secondary factors" two of which were clearly related to war/peace attitudes: punitiveness versus permissiveness and irresponsibility versus responsibility. These are shown in Figure 4, together with the various primary factors making up the two secondary factors. Figure 4 is a two-dimensional projection of what is essentially an 18-dimensional diagram. Since the punitiveness factor is independent of the responsibility factor, it is shown at right angles to it in the two-dimensional diagram. Other factors (e.g., religiosity, conservatism) which are correlated with punitiveness are shown as clustering around it—the higher the correlation the smaller the

Table 10

WAR/PEACE ATTITUDES AND PERSONALITY "PRIMARY FACTORS"

1. Militarism
Eckhardt's War Propaganda (1967)
Comrey's Nationalism (1965)
* Levy's Worldmindedness (1964)
Eysenck's Punitiveness (1955)
Laulicht's Military Forces (1965)
Laulicht's Anti-Communism (1965)
Comrey's Punitiveness (1965)
Eckhardt's Military Deterrence (1967)

2. Neuroticism
* Edward's Social Desirability (1966)
Eysenck's Neuroticism (1960)
Comrey's Neuroticism (1966)
Welsh's Anxiety (1960)
* Cattell's Ego Strength (1966)
* Comrey's Ascendence (1966)
MMPI Psychasthenia (1960)

Paul's Peace Responsibility (1963)
Laulicht's Foreign Aid (1965)

6. Misanthropy
Rosenberg's Misanthropy (1957)
White's Denunciation (1951)
Comrey's Hostility (1966)

7. Conservatism
Political Preference
Eysenck's Conservatism (1955)
Adorno's Conservatism (1950)
Comrey's Conservatism (1965)
Adorno's Ethnocentrism (1950)
Laulicht's Conservatism (1965)

8. Extraversion
MMPI Hypomania (1960)

3. Religiosity
Comrey's Religiosity (1965)
Cattell's Religious Sentiment (1960)
McLean's Religious Orthodoxy (1960)
Eysenck's Sex Morality (1955)
Allport's Religious Values (1951)
Religious Preference
* Eysenck's Toughmindedness (1955)
McLean's Fundamentalism (1960)

4. Social Responsibility
Gough's Social Responsibility (1960)
Cattell's Exploration (1960)
* Johns Hopkins's Alcoholism (1967)

5. Internationalism
Laulicht's United Nations (1965)

* Welsh's Repression (1960)
White's Egoistic Values (1951)
Bill's Self-assertive Values (1958)
Comrey's Rhathmia (1966)

9. Empathy
Comrey's Empathy (1966)

10. Nationalism
* Lentz' Worldmindedness (1950)

11. Discipline**
Itkin's Directive Discipline (1952)
* Eckhardt's Parental Praise (1968)
Eckhardt's Anxious Discipline (1968)
Eckhardt's Hypocritical Discipline (1968)
Itkin's Inconsistent Discipline (1952)

---

* negatively correlated

** only one discipline scale was used in the original study, but five scales were reported in later research (Eckhardt, 1969b).

Figure 4

TWO-DIMENSIONAL PROJECTION OF 18-DIMENSIONAL FACTOR DIAGRAM OF WAR/PEACE ATTITUDES

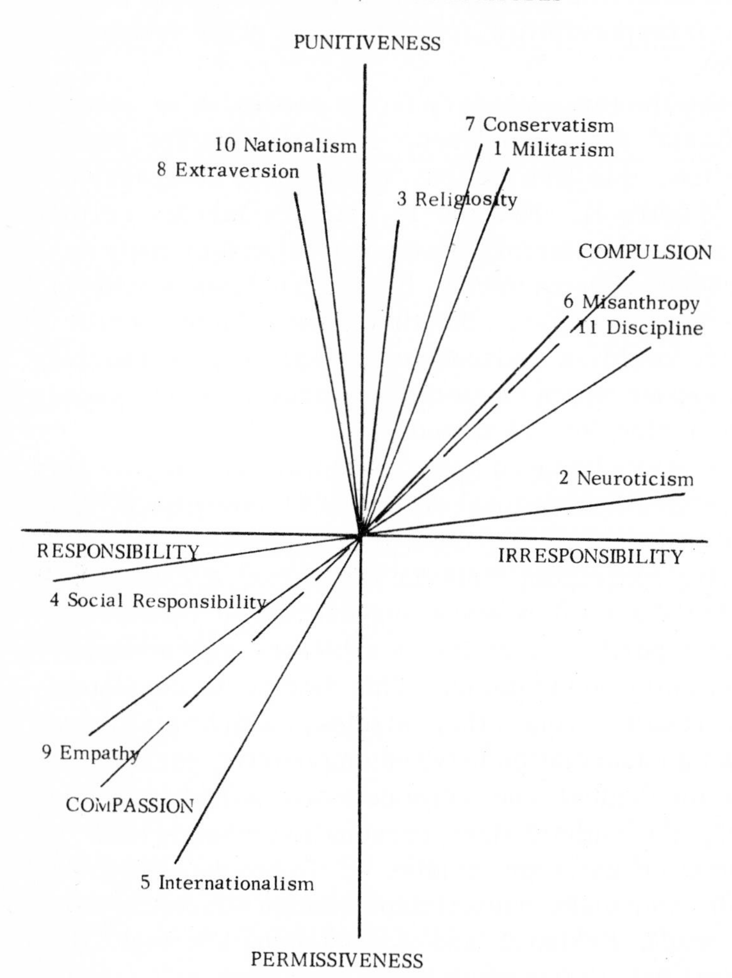

The more closely two factors are aligned, the more the attitudes or personality traits are associated with one another.

angle between the two arrows. Similarly the exploration factor correlates highly with the responsibility factor while the neuroticism factor correlates highly with irresponsibility (or negatively with responsibility).

When the two secondary factor scores were correlated and factor-analyzed, a single tertiary factor resulted; this was called "compulsion-compassion" (see Figure 4). Had the 18 primary factors or the five secondary factors been uncorrelated or truly independent of one another, further analysis would not have been possible. But they were related and ultimately could be reduced to a single comprehensive axis around which clustered so many of the personality and ideological attitudes.

The compulsion-compassion factor provides us not only with an operational definition of compulsion, but also with at least one clue to its origin. The strong positive correlation between this factor and recalled childhood discipline would suggest that compulsion is at least partly a function of arbitrary and/or unduly strict childhood training. This finding is consistent with results from other studies, which also have shown an association between compulsive variables—both ideological and personal—and strict training (e.g., the authoritarian personality investigation of Adorno, dogmatism studies of Rokeach (Rokeach, 1960) and many neuroticism studies since the time of Freud). Eckhardt and Alcock conclude that "the general value of compulsion is a function of an arbitrary, dogmatic, hypocritical, and/or unduly restrictive culture. Conversely, the general value of compassion is a function and expression of a more permissive and more rational culture." (Eckhardt and Alcock, 1970, p. 112.)

In social terms, the problems of poverty, prejudice and war seem to be functions of the relative value placed upon compulsion in any culture. To the extent that this is true, the solution of these problems will at least partly depend upon whether the culture will devalue compulsion and place a higher value on compassion. Not only must attitudes towards compassion change, but so must the culture's institutions, since institutions would mould attitudes.

CROSS-CULTURAL ATTITUDES

The previous study was Western-oriented, in fact it was North American-oriented. To overcome this fairly common bias, a group of scholars have recently cooperated in a world-wide measurement of war/peace attitudes. The multi-national student survey was designed by Finlay, Iversen, and Raser (1969), and administered by 42 researchers in 60 universities to over 5,000 male university students aged 22 to 24 in 18 nations from March 1968 to July 1969. The questionnaire which contained about 200 items was translated into 10 different languages.

A cross-cultural survey, one might think, would answer certain questions quite easily. Which countries are most nationalistic? or militaristic? or capitalistic? It would answer these questions if the respondents were a truly random sample of the people of each country. The Canadian survey previously reported (Chapter 7) was in fact such a study; this cross-cultural survey was not such a study. One step less reliable than a random sample of the whole population is a random sample of a select group of the population—of the students for example. Unfortunately, the survey reported here was not even that. While the Dutch questionnaires were from every university in the Netherlands, and the American questionnaires were from seven universities representing three broad regions in the country, most countries are represented by only two or three universities, and the questionnaires of two countries (West Germany and England) come from a single university. In spite of this limitation on accuracy, it is still reasonable to rank order the various countries according to the attitudes held into broad categories—high, medium, or low. At the worst, it gives us a measure of the attitudes of some future national leaders. Scale scores for some of the attitude variables are therefore reported for all of the countries tested.

An analysis of relationships between the various attitudes, however, is both feasible and reliable despite the non-random sample. Moreover, such an analysis is most likely to reveal whatever enduring differences there are between the different cultures. A number of correlation analyses have therefore been performed by one of the 42 researchers (Eckhardt, 1970[a,b,c], 1971.) Here is a brief review.

Four ideological factors had previously been singled out by Eckhardt and his co-workers: militarism, conservatism, religiosity and nationalism. In Western culture these four factors were so highly correlated that they formed a separate higher order factor, which Eckhardt labelled punitiveness (see Figure 4). He now raised the question: Would these four sets of attitudes be so highly correlated in other cultures? If not, in what way would they differ?

For convenience, the study arranged 15 of the 18 nations into five groups as follows: America (Australia, Canada, USA); Europe (England, Netherlands, West Germany); Scandinavia (Denmark, Sweden, Finland); Africa (Ghana, Nigeria, South Africa (black)); Asia (Ceylon, India, South Korea). The remaining three nations (Brazil, South Africa (white)), and an unnamed communist country) comprised an ill-assorted group and allowed few conclusions to be drawn, though their rank ordering will be reported later. The correlation analysis was performed by selecting an item to represent a given ideological factor (militarism, conservatism, religiosity, or nationalism) and correlating this item with all other relevant items for each group of nations. The following observations are based on the correlation coefficients—whether they were significant and whether they were positive or negative.

Conservatism was seen as the same thing for all groups of countries: a mixture of believing in the status quo ("The basic organization of our country should not be fundamentally changed."); faith in private property ("The institution of private property is a sound basis on which to build a society which fulfills the needs of its members.") and competition ("Competition is an effective way of promoting social progress."); Western orientation ("My country has more to learn from the West than from the East."); and a self-rating ("Compared with other students at your university or college, what would you say your political position is: to the left, about average, or to the right?"). But conservatism was not associated with as many other values in the East as it was in the West. In America, Europe and Scandinavia, conservatism positively correlated with nationalism, religiosity, militarism, racialism ("One of my primary loyalties is to my race.") and conformity ("It is important to me to follow rules and regulations closely."). Conservatism was also associated with religiosity in Asia and Africa, with militarism in Asia, and with conformity in Africa. But nationalists and racialists in Africa and Asia are as likely to be radical as conservative, while militarists in Africa and conformists in Asia are also as likely to be radicals as conservatives (see Figure 5).

The factor of militarism ("My country should not start to disarm.") produced the biggest surprise of all. As might be expected it correlated positively with nationalism, conservatism, religiosity, racialism and conformity in all three Western blocs: America, Europe, and Scandinavia. But militarism was negatively correlated with conformity in Asia and Africa and was negatively correlated with religiosity and racialism in Asia. In other words, the pacifists were the conformists in the East and not the non-conformists as in the West; equally surprising, those who believed in the worth of their religion and race in Asia (mostly Hindus and Buddhists) also believed in pacifism. Indeed, the only value which consistently was linked with militarism in all five regions of the world was nationalism.

Nationalism ("In the interests of peace, we must give up part of our national sovereignty." This item was then scored negatively) correlated positively not

Figure 5

CORRELATIONS BETWEEN MILITARISM, NATIONALISM, CONSERVATISM AND RELIGIOSITY FOR 18 NATIONS

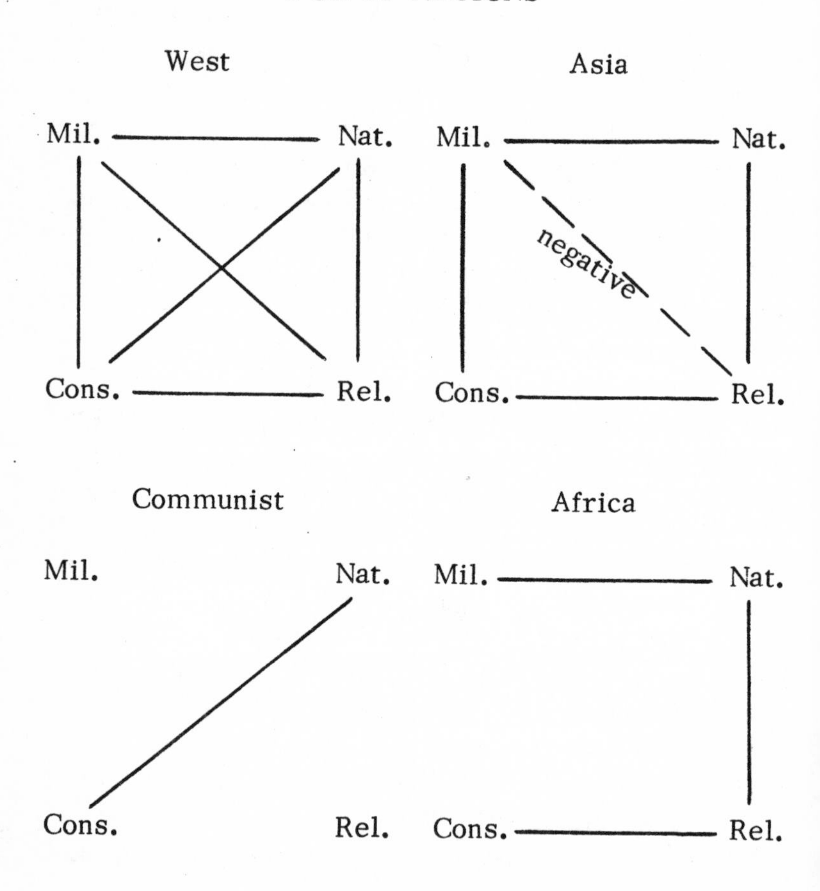

Table 11 - ATTITUDE RANK ORDERING OF 5,000 MALE UNIVERSITY STUDENTS (mean scale scores)

Rank	Conservatism	Militarism	Religiosity	Nationalism
	S. Africa (wh.)	S. Africa (wh.)	S. Africa (wh.)	Nigeria
	U.S.A.	India	S. Africa (bl.)	S. Korea
High	Sweden	S. Korea	Brazil	Ceylon
	Denmark	Nigeria	Ghana	Ghana
	Australia	Australia	Nigeria	India
	Finland	Finland	India	Brazil
	S. Korea	S. Africa (bl.)	Ceylon	S. Africa (wh.)
	Canada	Ceylon	Communist	S. Africa (bl.)
Medium	S. Africa (bl.)	Ghana	Finland	Australia
	Ghana	Brazil	S. Korea	U.S.A.
	Brazil	Canada	Netherlands	Canada
	Netherlands	U.S.A.	Australia	Finland
	England	Communist	England	Communist
	Communist	W. Germany	Sweden	England
Low	India	England	U.S.A.	Sweden
	W. Germany	Sweden	Canada	Denmark
	Nigeria	Netherlands	W. Germany	Netherlands
	Ceylon	Denmark	Denmark	W. Germany

only with militarism, but also with religiosity, conformity and racialism in America, Europe, Scandinavia, Asia and Africa—that is, in all groups tested. However, it did not correlate with conservatism in Asia or Africa, suggesting that radicals are as likely as conservatives to be nationalistic in the East.

Finally, religiosity ("The restraints imposed by strong religious institutions are essential to curb man's natural instincts.") was found to be positively related to all ideological variables in the West—America, Europe and Scandinavia. But, as already noted, it was opposed to militarism in Asia, and it was unrelated to militarism in Africa. This is especially interesting, since the religion most often given by students in each of the African countries—Ghana, Nigeria and South Africa (black)—was Christian. Apparently the missionaries taught them a different brand from their co-religionists in the West, or else their lessons did not "take."

Conservatism for the unnamed communist country meant a belief in capitalism and Western values in general, but it did not mean a belief in the status quo. It correlated with nationalism and religious affiliation but not with religiosity. Militarism was associated with conformity, but as in Africa it was unassociated with religiosity, conservatism or racialism. Militarism for the communist country, however, was not associated with nationalism. To summarize, among 293 students from three universities in an unnamed communist country, both radicals and conservatives are equally interested in armament or disarmament, but conservatives (who are Western-oriented and capitalistic) are the nationalists. Religiosity has little bearing on any other values.

To conclude, the attitude patterns around the world are basically similar to one another (over 60 percent of the total variance was accounted for by the first unrotated factor of a factor analysis of 90 different items). But there are important differences and we would do well not to gloss over what makes the other cultures dissimilar from Europe and North America. A belief in force in some underdeveloped parts of the world is not confined to conservatives and conformists. Equally enlightening, a belief in pacifism in some Asian countries is not confined to a few odd sects and the disbelievers as it is in the West, but is associated with the mainstream of their religion. In the newly-emerging ex-colonial countries of Africa and Asia nationalism and racialism are not necessarily linked to the conservative side of society, but are equally linked to the radicals.

Table 11 is a ranking of the mean scale scores for each of the attitudes we have discussed for the 5,000 male university students for 18 countries. What characterizes the high and low scores? A superficial reading suggests that wealth is a key criterion since over half of the highest ranking nations are poor whereas most of the lowest ranking nations are rich. An exception to this is conservatism since scale scores for conservatism are higher for the rich countries than they are for the poor countries. Poor countries rank higher than rich countries on militarism, however. Thus, while rich countries are more conservative, poor countries are much more nationalistic, religious and militaristic. An interesting conjecture, then, is that nationalism and militarism are very different for an exploited group than they are for the exploiters. Alternatively, poor nations who are often unstable former colonies may feel they have to arm against their neighbours. The communist country has medium religiosity, but low conservatism, nationalism and militarism which is consistent with the previous finding that of all four variables only nationalism and conservatism are linked.

PREJUDICE

In his Open and Closed Mind, psychologist Milton Rokeach has presented evidence that prejudice is in large part determined by a perceived dissimilarity of belief systems rather than by ethnic or racial membership. (Rokeach, 1960.) In his view a white southerner in the United States would feel much more kindly towards a coloured "Uncle Tom" who knew his place—that is, shared his belief that Negroes are inferior—than towards a white northerner who wanted equality for blacks. While Rokeach is not alone in his view, Gordon W. Allport in his classic The Nature of Prejudice maintains that there is no single cause of prejudice. He writes: "We may lay it down as a general law applying to all social phenomena that multiple causation is invariably at work and nowhere is the law more clearly applicable than to prejudice." (Allport, 1954, p. 218.)

Fresh light has been thrown on this age-old question by Harry C. Triandis and Earl E. Davis of the University of Illinois. (Triandis and Davis, 1965.) Triandis accepted the fact that friendship was determined by similarity of values and beliefs but hypothesized that prejudice involved negative behaviour as well and that race was the clue to some antagonistic behaviour. Three hundred white male students were asked to rate in a variety of ways eight hypothetical persons who represented all combinations of black-white, male-female and pro-anti strong civil rights legislation. When the questionnaires were analyzed, five factors emerged:

Formal social acceptance - I would cooperate in a political campaign, etc.

Marital acceptance - I would date, etc.

Friendship acceptance - I would eat with, etc.

Social distance - I would not accept as a close kin by marriage, etc.

Subordination - I would obey, etc.

The analysis determined the relative importance for each of the five factors of race, age, occupation, sex and religion. It was found that the relative weights given to race and belief are a function of the personality of the subject. One personality type was "conventionally" prejudiced, responding much more to the race than the beliefs of the hypothetical person, while the other personality type was more influenced by belief. For both types, however, the more intimate the hypothesized behaviour (marital acceptance and social distance), the larger the weight given to race. The less intimate the hypothesized behaviour (formal social acceptance), the more weight was given to beliefs, again for both personality groups. For the intermediate factors (friendship acceptance and subordination) the relative weight given to race or belief was in accord with the subject's personality.

Thus, in the case of intimate behaviour, Triandis'

arguments about race appear correct, while in the case of nonintimate behaviour (and international war would seem to fall in this category), Rokeach's arguments appear to be upheld. In the case of intermediate behaviour (civil rights and possibly civil war would seem to be included here) both race and belief are important. Due to their personalities, some subjects are more accurately described by Rokeach, others by Triandis, and behaviour intermediate between intimate and nonintimate is best able to distinguish between the two groups. Thus, in the matter of prejudice, both race and personality differences cannot be ignored; but as they apply to war, belief differences still remain paramount.

NATIONALISM

Race prejudice and nationalism were part of the punitiveness cluster of attitudes analyzed by Eckhardt. But how does a nationalistic attitude develop in a person?

According to David Easton and Robert D. Hess of the University of Chicago, the school is the formative agent, building upon earlier attitudes developed at home. "A child's political world," they state, "begins to take shape well before he even enters elementary school and undergoes the most rapid change during these years." (Easton & Hess, 1962, p. 235.) In one study, Easton and Jack Dennis surveyed 12,000 children from grades 2 to 8 in eight large cities in the United States. All children were from middle- or working-class districts. Both personal interviews and written questionnaires were used. The results might please some politicians, for the study found that the small child sees "a vision of holiness" when he glances in the direction of government. (Easton & Dennis, 1965, p. 43.) To the young child, the government is there to protect and care for him when he is in need. For the American school children sampled in grades 2 and 3, "government" signified an authority figure—either George Washington or the incumbent President—though "many children associate the sanctity and awe of religion with the political community. At ages 9 and 10, children sometimes have considerable difficulty in disentangling God and country." (Easton and Dennis, 1965.) Each morning in many schools it is customary to pledge allegiance "to the flag of the United States of America and to the Republic for which it stands, one nation under God, indivisible, with liberty and justice for all." The ritual is often reinforced by a prominently displayed picture of the President.

Only in the higher grades (7 and 8) did the personified image of government give way to a concept of Congress. The child therefore learns to like his government before he really knows what it is; overwhelmingly he sees the President as possessed "of all virtues and benign, wise, helpful, concerned for the welfare of others, protective, powerful, good and honest." (Easton and Dennis, 1965.) Apparently parents, in the United States at least, show a strong tendency to shelter children from the realities of political life. If the child is later to develop a more realistic view, then his discontent, cynicism or desire for change has to overcome an early high regard for his government.

But nationalism is an uneven commodity. Kenneth Terhune and his colleagues interviewed a sample of college students—average American and foreign students studying in the United States—to test their loyalties to themselves, their family, their province, country, continent and the world. (Terhune, 1965.) The investigators found that American college students rate their country high and the world low in their hierarchy of loyalties, though loyalty to family headed the list. Indian students rated the family high and the world low, but put loyalty to country at the head of the list. Canadian students, on the other hand, rated their family at the top and put loyalty to their country and the world at the bottom of the scale. If Canadian toddlers each day saluted the flag and were made more aware of their national leader, would their sense of nationalism change? We do not know, but it is reasonable to expect so. Or, if each day they saluted the U.N. flag and became aware of its Secretary-General, would they then develop a sense of loyalty to the world? Again, it seems reasonable to suppose so, and such an hypothesis could and should be tested.

Nationalism is an uneven commodity in another sense—within a country. The children of Cyprus studied their own history from two different textbooks: one for the Greek Cypriots, and one for the Turkish Cypriots. These two books were surprisingly similar—in reporting dates, events and causes—except for the smallest details. In one book it was carefully noted whenever the Turks burned down a cathedral upon entering a Cyprus town; in the second book the Greek sacking of mosques received comparable attention. (Education Advisory Committee of the Parliamentary Group for World Government, 1965.) In 1963, Cypriot children, grown to manhood, engaged in civil war.

9 economic evidence

An attitude study published by the Canadian Peace Research Institute strongly suggests that people are not worried about adverse economic effects in the event of disarmament. In general, they believe they will be able to keep their jobs. In the survey, 45 percent of the general public—and 58 percent of businessmen, 48 percent of labour leaders, 50 percent of politicians—thought that disarmament would lead to a minor recession or depression. More than half of the general public who thought so also believed that "advanced planning by our governments and business leaders would avoid it." (Paul and Laulicht, 1963.) This opinion was shared by 57 percent of businessmen, 67 percent of labour leaders and 68 percent of politicians. Their conclusion is further confirmed, in the United States, by a *New York Times* survey of 25 prime defence contractors who handle 51 percent of all defence work. They were asked what plans they had made for the possibility of an arms control or disarmament agreement. Though few were planning for arms cutbacks and "two companies would not even discuss the problem," most "contractors felt they could manage the difficult transition required." (The Globe and Mail, August 19, 1963.) The same conclusion was reached by the Senate Foreign Relations Subcommittee on Disarmament when in 1962 it carried out a confidential survey of firms involved in United States defence. "Not one of these companies ... opposed a disarmament agreement on (economic) grounds." (War/Peace Report, November, 1962, p. 21.)

How realistic is this widespread opinion that disarmament would not cause serious economic difficulties?

Fortunately, economic studies have been done in a number of nations, so expert confirmation of this point of view can be given with some confidence. This was not the case 12 years ago. Peace Research Abstracts lists more than 982 entries in its "Economics of Disarmament" section, of which only 6 percent were published before 1960. (Peace Research Abstracts, Volumes I, II, III.)

In 1962 a consultative group of experts from the United States, Soviet Union, United Kingdom and seven other governments reported to the United Nations that the world was spending roughly $120 billion on armaments annually; this represented about 8-9 percent of the world's annual output. Seven countries (United States, Soviet Union, China, United Kingdom, France, West Germany and Canada) accounted for 85 percent of the total, with the United States and the Soviet Union alone accounting for 70 percent. The experts concluded, however, that a recession following disarmament could be prevented now in both private enterprise and centrally planned economies.

(Patel, 1962.)

UNITED STATES

Since it is more difficult to predict the actions of a private enterprise economy, it may be worthwhile to look in detail at the effect disarmament might produce in the United States. Emile Benoit, Kenneth Boulding and 13 other economists in the first major study of American disarmament provide some tentative but guardedly optimistic answers to this question. (Benoit and Boulding, 1963.) They feel there are two problems: first, maintaining adequate overall demand for the new goods and services into whose production the defence resources will be rechannelled; secondly, overcoming obstacles to a prompt and smooth shift of the displaced resources into new uses. Having carefully considered these twin problems, the economists conclude:

> Our economy is remarkably capable of overcoming structural obstacles in the presence of adequate overall demand. This was well demonstrated, both during World War II and in the period immediately after it, when enormous changes in labor force, in industrial skill patterns, and even in regional distribution of population occurred with startling rapidity and extraordinarily little friction and hardship....
>
> While structural problems, therefore, possess an independent importance, they are, nevertheless of clearly subordinate significance when compared to the fundamental problem of main-

taining adequate demand. (Benoit, 1963, p. 286.)

But maintaining aggregate demand is not easy. As Benoit points out:

> We face a difficult unemployment situation in the 1960s, with a rapid growth of the labor force, and accelerated labor displacement from automation.... Industrial output, which had risen 6 percent from 1951 to 1953, rose only 2.6 percent a year from 1953 to 1961. The unemployment rate rose from 3 percent to a post-Korean War average of 5.4 percent....
>
> Indeed, the disturbing aspect of the economic adjustment to the post-Korean (War) defense cuts was the industrial slow-down. If there were a new industrial slow-down in conjunction with disarmament in the 1960s and 1970s, it could be dangerous both to internal morale and external prestige. (Benoit, 1963, pp. 274-5.)

The post-Korean (War) cutbacks occurred during a 7-year period; the disarmament cutbacks envisaged in this study would take place over a 12-year period and are less precipitous.

To the Swedish economist Gunnar Myrdal, however, this relatively slow growth in the United States since 1953 is part of a cyclic pattern of recessions and sharp upturns resulting from an absence of coordinated national planning. (Myrdal, 1963.) Thus, the economic problem of disarmament would be an additional aggravation to an already distressed economy. It is therefore important to the world, Myrdal believes, to get the United States economy growing more rapidly. His remedy for the peacetime economy is the same as that advocated by Benoit for a transition to disarmament—more public spending by government. But the two economists are divided on how best to invest the government's money. Mydral advocates increased spending for education, medical care and slum clearance; Benoit, in turn, recommends that revenues be used to develop disarmament inspection techniques and to further the space program. Both economists are agreed, however, on one potential U.S. investment—a program of world economic development. While these steps may be practical and economically feasible, it is unlikely that they would prove acceptable politically in a nation which, ideologically committed to capitalism, regards public spending by government is a necessary evil rather than a necessary good. Herein may lie the greatest obstacle to disarmament.

Disarmament in the United States, of course, would have worldwide repercussions. "International trade changes after disarmament," the United States Arms Control and Disarmament Agency notes, "would right the U.S. balance of payments ... but might have some adverse effects on some primary producers such as some countries in Asia and Africa and in Canada." (U.S. Arms Control: Disarmament Agency, 1962.)

CANADA

The effect of disarmament—both Canadian disarmament and American disarmament—on the Canadian economy has been studied by Gideon Rosenbluth. (Rosenbluth, 1967.) Canadian disarmament is easy, compared to that of the United States, since less than half as much per capita is spent on defence in Canada. American disarmament would affect both the primary and secondary producers in Canada, but Rosenbluth does not believe the effect would be serious.

Nevertheless a special problem remains; industrial, occupational and regional mobility is less in Canada than in many other countries. A regression analysis carried out by Rosenbluth suggests that cities of less than 100,000 inhabitants are less "elastic" with respect to employment than the larger centers and that detailed case studies of selected towns and cities should be made. By contrast, the resultant reduction in Gross National Product for Canada, as a result of disarmament—even under the rather rapid 5-year plan suggested by the Russians at the Eighteen Nation Disarmament Committee in Geneva in 1962—would be no cause for concern, being less than 1 percent per annum. "Given a modicum of planning," Rosenbluth concludes, "the reconversion task accompanying disarmament should present no difficulty." (Rosenbluth, 1967.)

UNITED KINGDOM

In the United Kingdom, the situation is even more sanguine. According to a study done by the Economic Intelligence Unit, the United Kingdom should be able to make a complete change to a peaceful economy, if properly planned, within 2 years. (Economist Intelligence Unit, 1963.) It should be noted, however, that

Benoit deems this an over-optimistic appraisal of the time needed for the British economy to adjust to disarmament; otherwise, Benoit commends the study for its professional competence.

10 evidence from political science

The first group of studies discussed in this chapter is, in one sense, an extension of Richardson's work because there is the same attempt to relate various national characteristics to the likelihood of war. More recent data (1900-1960) and more sophisticated statistical techniques—mainly factor analysis—are employed in these later studies, which also go beyond Richardson in looking closely at the "societal" conditions of a nation; that is, internal features of a large system composed of many social groups within a fixed territorial boundary. Richardson concentrated more on "social" conditions; that is, the effects of personal characteristics like language, religion or dress.

The following could be considered as societal conditions important to the study of conflict: authoritarianism, economic depressions, revolutions, number of riots, assassinations, homicides, deaths due to alcoholism and suicides. Also important are: the wealth of a nation, its population, urbanization and rate of social change. How do these factors affect the likelihood of a nation's going to war?

FOREIGN STRIFE

In an attempt to shed light on this complicated question, R. J. Rummel and Raymond Tanter analyzed the behaviour of 77 nations from 1955 to 1957, and of 83 nations from 1958 to 1960. (Rummel, 1966, Tanter, 1966.) Each man considered nine variables indicative of domestic strife (e.g., purges, revolutions, riots) and 13 variables indicative of foreign strife (e.g., diplomatic protests, recall of ambassadors, mobilization of troops, actual war).

Their information was obtained largely from the New York Times, but three other publications also were used: Deadline Data on World Affairs, Britannica Book of the Year and Facts on File. While some bias is certain to be introduced by the pro-Western nature of the sources, the method of analysis is free of such criticism.

In the first part of the double study, the 13 foreign strife variables were found to cluster into three categories or factors, each of which was independent of, or unrelated to, the other two: "diplomatic" (numbers of ambassadors recalled or expelled); "belligerency" (severance of diplomatic relations); and "war" (numbers of people killed in war). In brackets after each factor is the most important foreign strife variable making up that factor.

In the second part of the study, the nine domestic strife variables were found by Rummel to cluster around three independent factors: "turmoil" (riots, acts of terrorism, etc.); "revolutions" (mutinies, coups, plots, etc.); and "civil war." Tanter recognized only two independent factors—turmoil and revolution were strongly correlated.

In the third and most significant part of the study, the three foreign factors and the two (or three) domestic factors were analyzed together to see if belligerent foreign policy actions of a nation are in part dependent on domestic strife conditions. Both factor and multiple regression analyses were used.

The resulting correlations were small: only 8 percent of the total variance of the foreign strife factors (that is, 8 percent of all the variables needed) was accounted for by the domestic strife factors in Tanter's study, and only 4-7 percent in Rummel's. Both figures are too low to be significant. Domestic conditions apparently are not reflected in foreign policy; nor does foreign policy affect domestic conditions. The regression analysis was run both ways—with one unexpected result. When the 1955-57 domestic data were used to predict foreign wars in 1958-60, 12 percent of the variance was accounted for (a correlation of 0. 34). Though a correlation of 0. 34 is not large, it approaches significance. The implication is that domestic turmoil today may be a partial cause of war tomorrow. One is reminded of Richardson's query: Was the great depression of 1929 a precipitating cause of World War II in 1939?

Another unexpected relationship was revealed when the Tanter and Rummel results were studied by another investigator, Michael Haas. (Haas, 1965.) Haas reports on the results of his own work and reviews that of Rummel and Tanter, Raymond Cattell, and Arthur Banks, Robert Textor and Phillip Gregg. The conclusions of this review are shown in Table 12. Gregg and Banks report that foreign conflict is independent of the authoritarianism of a country. But after analyzing their data in a somewhat different fashion, Haas reports "a slight but consistent tendency for democratic countries to have less foreign conflict than undemocratic political systems." His result is shown in Table 12 as a qualified "yes."

A recent study by Dean V. Babst (1970) strongly supports Haas' tentative conclusion. "There are certain kinds of government that do not fight each other," according to Babst, "and these are the independent freely elected governments." From 1841 to 1941, the period covered in the study, the number of such independent freely elected governments grew from two to more than 40. Using Wright's data (1942), Babst considered the 76 major wars and 278 warring countries. His conclusion: while many of the elected governments fought against "autocratic" governments or against their own colonies who were trying to become independent, none of them fought against each other. A causal relationship, of course, has not been definitely established by the study; other factors may be at work—common ideology for example. Nevertheless, with a correlation which is so significant (of over 40 nations, none has fought one another) one must conclude that democracy itself is a pacifying agent.

A correlation between the wealth of a nation and foreign conflict was not found in the Gregg and Banks data. Cattell, however, found a "cultural pressure" factor which had significant positive correlations with standard of living (.35), per capita income (.34) and foreign war (.62); while Haas showed that national wealth, using United Nations' assessment as an esti-

Table 12

CORRELATION OF DOMESTIC SOCIETAL CONDITIONS WITH FOREIGN CONFLICT

Domestic Societal Conditions	Investigator			
	Rummel and Tanter	Haas	Cattell	Banks, Textor and Gregg
authoritarianism		(yes)		no
wealth		yes	yes	no
unemployment		yes	no	
revolution	no	no		
riots	no	yes		yes
homicide		no	no	
suicide		yes	yes	
population density		no	no	
urban population density		yes	yes	

mate, is significantly correlated with foreign conflict.

No relationship between unemployment and war was found in Cattell's analysis (during a limited period of years), but from 1900 to 1960 Haas found that unemployment and frequency of war had a small positive correlation of 0.33.

Tanter and Rummel had concluded that domestic strife was independent of foreign conflict. Suspicious of this result, particularly in view of the time-lag effect, Haas subjected their data to a further test. Their nine domestic variables were regrouped into "legitimate" conflict (strikes, government crises), "illegitimate" conflict (revolution and purges) and "anomic" conflict (riots and demonstrations). With this change, the domestic variables comprising the "anomic" group (with only one exception) were found to correlate positively with each of the foreign conflict variables. On the other hand, only 76 percent of the variables comprising the "legitimate" and "illegitimate" groups correlated positively with each of the foreign strife variables. The difference between 76 percent for the legitimate and illegitimate groups and 98 percent for the anomic group may be important, because, says Haas, "consistence of results is often more important for social theory than the significance or magnitude of overall findings." Moreover, according to Haas, the same consistency of results shows up in the Banks and Textor data relating to anomic groups.

Riots, demonstrations, revolutions and purges are examples of active deviance (see Glossary) aimed at the rules governing social and political behaviour. Active deviance directed at persons, rather than at rules or institutions, commonly takes the form of assault, from fistfights to homicides. Both Cattell and Haas tested for a correlation between foreign conflict and homicide rates but found none.

If, however, regulations and rules are seen by an individual as a source of his frustration, which he cannot change, he may seek some form of escape from social reality. He may engage in such forms of passive deviance as suicide or the use of narcotics or alcohol. Alcoholism was found by Cattell and by Haas to be negligibly linked to war, but both investigators report that suicide is positively correlated with foreign strife.

Haas' study shows that, while a country's average population density is unrelated to foreign conflict, high urban population density (percent of population in cities of 20,000 or more) is related to war. It is of interest, then, that in the Cattell study population density had only a .32 loading (just significant) on the "cultural pressure" factor, while "urbanization" had a loading of .78. The cultural pressure factor itself, it will be recalled, correlated with foreign war.

It appears from these various analyses that urbanization relates to nearly all the factors contributing to foreign conflict; e.g., wealth, unemployment, riots, suicide and high population. Unfortunately few of the correlations reported are high, so the consistency of the findings is of more significance than each individual result.

In an earlier chapter we quoted Elton B. McNeil: "Man's animal nature is a feeble excuse for violence." It now seems appropriate to finish the quotation: "A more reasonable explanation is that the seemingly senseless violence of human beings may be one of the costs of urban living." (McNeil, 1966, p. 151.) Unlike McNeil, Konrad Lorenz assigns to man's animal nature the major role in accounting for human aggression, while conceding: "That crowding increases the propensity to aggressive behavior has long been known and demonstrated experimentally by sociological research." (Lorenz, 1966, p. 253.) The findings reported in this chapter would seem to support both McNeil's and Lorenz' contentions that a disposition towards war depends at least in part on urban stress.

A remarkable example of the dangers of crowding, however, is the 1969 war between El Salvador and Honduras. (Ehrlich, Paul, 1970, p. 311.) Tiny El Salvador, with a population of 3.3 million persons, had a population density of 782 persons per square mile of arable land; by contrast, Honduras had only 155 persons per square mile of arable land. In consequence, 300,000 Salvadors moved into neighbouring Honduras in search of land and jobs. Friction developed between the native Hondurans and immigrant Salvadors and the problem escalated into a brief but nasty war. Subsequently, the Organization of American States recognized the demographic factor in its formula for settling the dispute. This example is all the more remarkable and significant since by other criteria—arms levels and arms build-up—the two countries would predictably have been extremely peaceful (see later in this chapter for the predictive value of armaments).

Crowding, however, may be a symptom of another stress, that of a recently imposed disorganization.

The disturbing effect on rhesus monkeys of a drastic change of territory has already been noted. The ethologist J. P. Scott has argued that poor adaptation to new surroundings can also lead to aggression among humans. "The majority of crimes are committed in an interval when a man is no longer under family control and generally has not yet formed his own family—in other words, the period of maximum family and social disorganization." (Genovés, 1970, p. 64.) Perhaps we all yearn simply to know our place and our space.

FOREIGN RELATIONS

Theoretical models of biological, physical or social systems are examples of deductive science, that is, they postulate a relationship which can be tested experimentally (see Chapter 6). Alternatively and more commonly, science can be inductive. Quantitative data are amassed and then an effort is made to simplify the data by means of mathematical relationships. The relationships, equations, or formulas may explain the phenomena or they may not, but at least they are in the direction of greater understanding. Whenever there is a source of "hard" data, that is, reasonably accurate figures, there is a strong temptation for any scientist to fit them into some kind of theoretical framework.

Recently two sources of hard data have become available and, in consequence, numerous attempts have been made to "explain" these figures. The two sets of figures are the General Assembly roll-call voting record of the hundred-odd countries at the

United Nations, and annual armament expenditures for these same countries.

In order to separate nations into groups on the basis of their U.N. voting records, it is convenient to use the method of factor analysis. Peace researchers Hanna Newcombe, Michael Ross and Alan Newcombe (1969) divided the 25 General Assembly Sessions from 1945 to 1969 into five separate periods and subjected each period to a Q-mode factor analysis in order to determine which nations normally cluster together. Had another type of factor analysis (R-mode) been used, clusters of voting issues (admission of China, colonialism, cold war, etc.) rather than clusters of nations would have emerged. But why mathematical methods? Surely it is obvious which nations regularly vote together and which issues are most important? Newcombe and her colleagues answered this reasonable query by postulating a British Commonwealth bloc on the basis of tradition. In fact, the computer check showed that the Commonwealth shows "no trace of voting together." The members of the Old Commonwealth vote with the West or the Imperial bloc, while the New Commonwealth votes with other Afro-Asians.

The results of the United Nations' analysis are as follows: there were 58 nations in period 1 (1946-50); 60 nations in period 2 (1951-55); 81 nations in period 3 (1956-59); 99 nations in period 4 (1960-63); and 115 nations in period 5 (1965-69). No votes were cast in 1964 due to a stalemate over financing the Congo operations. Only two clusters of nations persisted throughout the whole period: a West bloc and a Soviet bloc. The percentage of nations in the West bloc diminished from 73 percent of the total number of nations in period 1 to 46 percent in period 5; at the same time the number of nations in the Soviet bloc increased from 10 percent in period 1 to 38 percent in period 5. The Afro-Asians comprised a separate bloc throughout periods 1 to 3, but merged with the Soviet bloc in periods 4 and 5. Scandinavia was part of the West bloc in period 1, but formed a bloc of its own in all other periods. The Latin American nations formed a bloc of their own in periods 1 and 2, but merged with the West in periods 3 to 5. An Imperial bloc separated from the West in period 3 but rejoined them in periods 4 and 5. Finally, a pro-West neutral bloc split off from the West bloc in periods 3 to 5. The authors conclude that there is a trend towards increasing bipolarization: the Latin Americans joined the West, while the Afro-Asians joined the Soviet bloc. Though the voting patterns of the two main blocs are not in sharper disagreement, each has drawn in new members to its ranks.

What characteristics do the nations within a U.N. voting bloc have in common? To answer this question, Alcock and Greenfield (1970) did a multiple regression analysis of each of the five main blocs—West, Soviet, Afro-Asian, Latin American, and Scandinavian—over three time periods: 1951-55, 1956-59, and 1960-63. Bloc members were those determined by Newcombe, et al., and the correlation matrix upon which the analysis was based also came from the earlier study. A multiple regression analysis is based on one dependent variable and a number of independent variables. The dependent variable used in this study was the correlation coefficient between any pair of voting nations. On the basis of earlier work by other investigators, Alcock and Greenfield used as independent variables: percent domestic communist votes, percent domestic socialist votes, percent Roman Catholics, GNP per capita, population density, population, geographic distance between national capitals. Each was thought to have some influence on how one country might "view" another. Countries chosen as representing their blocs were respectively: the U.S.A., U.S.S.R., India, Brazil and Sweden. All of the independent variables except geographic distance were taken from the World Handbook of Political and Social Indicators (1964) and were therefore for the years 1957-62. Strictly speaking it would have been better to alter the values of the predictor variables as they changed over time, but in practice the changes would have been nominal. Regression equations were determined for the three time periods based on the "distance" of each of the bloc representatives from all other countries for the different variables. For example, Israel might be close to the U.S.S.R. in GNP per capita and percent Roman Catholics, but distant in percent communist votes or geographically. To the extent that any of these independent variables influenced the dependent variable, it would show up in the coefficients of the resulting regression equation. A separate equation was determined for each bloc for each of the three time periods.

The results can be summarized as follows. There was little change over the three time periods. Four variables proved to have considerable predictive value, namely: GNP per capita, percent communist votes, percent socialist votes, and geographic distance between capitals. The remaining three variables had little if any additional predictive capability: population, population density, and percent Roman Catholics. For each bloc over the whole time period, only two predictive terms seemed to be necessary, and the two terms were in each case characteristic of that bloc. For the nations of the West bloc, whether another nation is thought of as a trusted friend or a dangerous adversary depends almost entirely on how many people in that country voted communist (bad), modified only slightly by whether the country was rich (good). The Soviet bloc was only in part a mirror image of the West. For them it was also of prime importance to know how many communists (good) there were, but it was almost as important to know what percent of the people voted socialist (bad), according to the results of this study. The Scandinavians apparently see their friends as socialist and rich, one being as vital as the other. For the Afro-Asians, on the other hand, the rich nations were the ones to distrust, on the basis of their U.N. voting record, while geographic distance also lent disenchantment. Their friends, apparently, were the poor and nearby nations of the world, and this fact was uppermost in their minds when they cast their U.N. votes. Finally, though the Latins departed from their friends in the West on geographic grounds, they too were committed to anti-communism. These four variables do not account for all of a nation's voting habits at the United Nations (half of the variance is accounted for by the two-term equations) but certainly they are a strong influence. The authors concluded: U.N. voting in the General Assembly appears to be a sensitive indicator of ideological and/or class differences between nations.

ARMAMENTS

Why does a nation arm? Richardson postulated ambition (or grievance) and fear of a neighbouring power when he created his arms race equations. Smoker attempted to go further with his polarization coefficients by introducing a numerical measure of the neighbours' intentions—to what extent were they friendly or hostile?

With the publication in 1969 of an extensive and consistent set of armament expenditures for the nations of the world (the SIPRI Yearbook of World Armaments and Disarmament 1968/69), it has become easy to pursue the question: why does a nation arm? Newcombe (1969), for example, plotted the 1966 military expenditures of 103 nations (rank order) versus GNP (rank order) and found that warring nations generally were above average in ratio of military expenditure to GNP (as might be expected) and that island nations—no borders—tended to be below average in arms spending, lending support to Richardson's finding that numbers of borders correlated with tendency to war.

Alcock (1970) sought to identify those independent variables which might predict the likelihood of a nation's arming. On the basis of conclusions drawn by a number of earlier investigators, he hypothesized that the threat perceived by a nation depends on the number of contiguous neighbours, on the ideological and/or class differences between these neighbours and the nation concerned, and on the relative power of the neighbours, and that perceived threat leads to increased military expenditure (hypothesis 1). He further hypothesized that military expenditure incurred to meet the perceived threat increased the probability of war (hypothesis 2). Hypothesis 1 was tested by means of a multiple regression analysis of 42 (non-warring) nations; all variables were in rank order form. The dependent variable was military expenditure as a percent of GNP for the year 1960. Independent variables were number of bordering countries, ideological and/or class distance of the neighbouring nation with the greatest ideological and/or class difference, power distance of the neighbouring country most nearly equal in power, and GNP/capita. National powers were assumed equal to energy consumption; ideological and/or class distance was based on the correlation coefficients between pairs of nations in the United Nations for roll-call votes of all the 1955-59 regular plenary sessions of the General Assembly (as determined by Newcombe, et al., 1969).

Hypothesis 1 was partly confirmed: military expenditure as a percent of GNP was dependent on perceived threat—43 percent of the variance being accounted for—where perceived threat was defined as the ideological and/or class difference between a nation and its most threatening neighbour. The military expenditure of a country as a percent of its GNP was also dependent on its economic development (GNP /capita), that is to say, five percent of GNP going to arms is less serious for a rich country than it is for a poor country. In this study, military spending was not found to be dependent on either power differences between neighbours or on numbers of neighbours. Since the more neighbours one has, the more chance there is of one of them being ideologically very different, this last finding is consistent with earlier research.

Hypothesis 2—that a high and growing armament budget increases the chance of war—was tested by correlating military expenditure (in 1960) and rate of increase of military expenditure (1961-64) for 86 non-warring nations with war casualties in the 1964-69 period. The hypothesis was confirmed since the probability of war was positively correlated almost equally with arms expenditure as a fraction of GNP and with rate of increase of arms expenditure. The correlations, however, were low—0.30 in each case. 11 nations went to war though they had been predicted as peaceful, another 11 nations did not go to war though they had been predicted as war-like; but eight nations for whom conflict was predicted subsequently engaged in conflict—UAR, Saudi Arabia, Israel, Iraq, Australia, Somalia, Lebanon, and the Netherlands. All were involved in <u>international</u> conflict. On the other hand, six of the 11 nations for whom war was unexpected were involved in <u>civil</u> war. Also notable was the finding that of the 11 nations which were unexpectedly peaceful, five had a high standard of living.

No significant correlation was found between ideological and/or class difference and war casualties. In fact, hypotheses 1 and 2 can be summarized as follows: <u>ideological and/or class differences between nations and sufficient wealth to support a weapons system are causative factors of high arms levels;</u>

while high arms levels and high rates of increase of arms levels are together causative factors of international war. Stated in another way, two steps seem to be involved: a nation which has an attitude for war is more likely to develop a power for war, and a power for war increases the probability of war, but an attitude for war alone does not increase the probability of war. Arms races thus seem to be both a symptom and a cause of tension.

These conclusions were further tested by Alcock through the use of a composite international "threat" index (1971a). Military expenditures as a percent of GNP (1966), rate of increase of military expenditure (1964-66), and (negatively) GNP/capita (1966) were listed for 117 nations. The three indices were first put into rank order form and, after the military expenditure term had been given double weight, were added together to make up a final "threat" index. This index was then compared with actual international conflict over a seven-year period (1964-70). The top half or high threat portion of the list contained 23 nations already engaged in international war in 1964-66. Another 34 countries were predicted to be likely to engage in international war—20 of them subsequently did in the 1967-70 period. The bottom half or low threat portion of the list contained eight nations already engaged in international war in 1964-66. Another 52 were predicted to be unlikely to engage in international war—only four subsequently did in 1967-70. To conclude, 20 out of 24 or 83 percent of all nations which were involved in international conflict over a four-year time period were successfully predicted by means of a three-term formula. 48 out of 62 or 77 percent of all nations which did not engage in international violence over the same period were correctly predicted. The formula accounted for approximately 47 percent of the total variance. Part of the missing variance may have been population pressure since two of the four nations which "unexpectedly" went to war were El Salvador and Honduras (see page 144).

Further evidence of the value of arms spending for predicting international war comes from an historical study. Political scientist Michael D. Wallace (1970), using data from the Correlates of War project (Singer, Small and Jones), performed a multiple regression analysis of 25 nations from 1820 to 1945. The dependent variable was international war. It was measured by the number of battle-related fatalities from international wars of magnitude greater than 3.0 which started during any given five-year period, the time interval used for the study. The independent variables—rates of change of population, increases in armament levels, rates of change of diplomatic status, rates of change of alliances, and rates of change of intergovernmental organization—were all derived from the primary data: total population, size of regular armed forces, number of diplomatic missions, etc.

Several of Wallace's findings seem especially significant:

(a) of all the variables, alliances affect armed forces levels the most and armed forces increases lead directly to war; but alliances do not lead to war directly;

(b) intergovernmental organizations have a slight

tendency to inhibit arms build-ups, but at least over the past century, this role would seem to be unimportant;

(c) increases in armed forces levels have a powerful and direct effect on international war. In fact, it is the only variable in the analysis which always affects war directly, the other variables in general being only the first step of a two-step process.

Wallace concludes: "Arms levels would appear to be the key factor in transforming the tensions generated by the structure of the international system into open belligerency. This would appear to discredit the widely-held theory that armaments are not of themselves a cause of war, but only reflect tensions generated by other factors which are the true causes."

ARMS RACES

Can arms spending, which so successfully predicts which nations are going to war, tell us when nations might turn to violence? Alcock, Young, and Kielly (1971) thought it might. The method they used was typal analysis, a young cousin of factor analysis. A type is defined as a set of nations, each one of which is more highly correlated with some other nation in that set than it is correlated with any nation outside of that set. The basic data, then, is a correlation matrix linking together all the nations being analyzed. Defence expenditures could have been used for the analysis; instead, the rates of change of defence expenditures were used since they were found in a preliminary calculation to be more sensitive indicators.

The authors were looking for regularities: first, between nations—how many arms races are there in the world; secondly, over time—do arms races follow regular patterns? Finally, they wished to assess whether or not any rhythms of arms expenditures were linked to the rhythms of war.

The fact that war is periodic over time was first noted by J. E. Moyal (1949) and later confirmed by Frank Denton (1966) and J. David Singer and Melvin Small. Moyal used Quincy Wright's list of wars from 1480 to 1900 to test two hypotheses. His first hypothesis states that the number of wars in a given period correlates with the number of wars in a past period separated by a fixed interval. He found for the outbreak of war that time lags of five and 15 years were significant. Moyal's second hypothesis was that there is a slow oscillation in the outbreak of war. He found this to be so with a period from peak to peak in numbers of wars of about 200 years. Using Richardson's list of wars from 1820 to 1949, Denton looked for time patterns in the "amount of violence." The amount-of-violence index was a composite of number of wars, number of casualties, and the number of participants. He found a periodicity of 25 years. When the study was later extended to the larger time period of 420 years covered by Wright's data, the time period was found to be about 20 years prior to 1695 and 30 years thereafter. There also appeared to be a saw-tooth pattern of violence (slow rise, rapid descent) which recurs about every 100 years. Singer, Small, and Jones (1969), on the basis of their own carefully compiled data covering the years from 1816 to 1965, did not find a short (5 year) or very long (100 to 200 year) periodicity, but did confirm "a clear 20-year periodicity between peaks in the amount of war underway at any given time." They found no rhythm in the onset of war (1969).

Against this background of historical evidence for war cycles Alcock, Young and Kielly scrutinized the post-World War II period from 1945 to 1970. Annual defence differences (in 1960 prices) were calculated for 51 nations from 1949 to 1969, for 58 nations from 1954 to 1969, and for 95 nations from 1960 to 1969. Typal analysis of the correlation matrices revealed three types of nations which persisted over all time periods: (1) a large East-West bloc, mainly comprising members of NATO, the Warsaw Pact and the OAS; (2) a medium-sized Middle East bloc mainly comprising Israel and Arab League members; (3) a small Far East bloc mainly comprising SEATO members. Arms expenditures of all three groups were found to be increasing with time over the past decade. Moreover, in at least one of the time periods studied all groups included one pair of belligerent nations. One of the aims of the study was therefore achieved—national defence budgets can prove the existence of arms races.

A second aim of the study was to detect regularities with respect to time. Annual defence increments for several nations from each of the three blocs were plotted over a 20-year period. This was followed by trial-and-error curve fitting, using a variety of sine waves and exponentials or arithmetic combinations of the two. Finally, the defence increments of all nations were correlated with the three curves which by inspection appeared to give the best fit to the three types of nations. This proved rewarding since each curve correlated only with the nations of one bloc with two exceptions—the United States and the United Kingdom. Though they were part of the East-West bloc, they correlated as well with the Far East bloc curve over the 20-year period. The second aim of the study was therefore achieved. Three cycles emerged (each associated with one of the arms races) with sinusoidal periods of 5.3 years (East-West); 2.7 years (Middle East), and 6.8 years (Far East). One of the arms races—the Middle East—exhibits an exponential rise which in fact dominates the cyclic pattern. Not all nations correlate significantly with the sinusoidal patterns, but some do for all periods studied and others correlate some of the time. For example, of the 58 countries studied over the 15-year period, 35 countries were part of one of the three arms race blocs while 18 were correlated significantly with one of the three arms race curves. These results are shown in Table 13.

Part three of the arms race study was an investigation to see if the likelihood of war was associated with the arms race rhythms. The 37 countries which had periodicities in their arms expenditures (that is, those countries which correlated with curves A, B, or C during any of the three time periods studied) were checked for conflict in the post-World War II period: 1945-70. Conflicts in which they were involved were listed under the appropriate heading: East-West, Middle East, or Far East. Two separate lists were made, one including conflicts of any size and another including only the larger wars—greater than magnitude 3.0 (Richardson rating) for Middle

Table 13

ARMS RACES IN THE 1954-1969 PERIOD
(as determined by typal analysis)

East-West

Nation	Correlation with Curve A (5.3 year period)
U.S.A.	.65
U.K.	
France	.49
Canada	.49
Netherlands	
Ireland	
Denmark	
Finland	
U.S.S.R.	
Czechoslovakia	.67
South Africa	
Spain	.58
Portugal	.51
Mexico	
Brazil	
Peru	.70
Honduras	.55
El Salvador	.60
Colombia	
Guatemala	
Chile	
Lebanon	
Japan	

Middle East

Nation	Correlation with Curve B (2.7 year period)
Israel	.89
U.A.R.	.81
Syria	.59
Jordan	.70
Greece	.70
Philippines	.81
South Korea	

Far East

Nation	Correlation with Curve C (6.8 year period)
New Zealand	.60
Malaysia	.42
Pakistan	
Iraq	.44
Sudan	

East arms race belligerents or greater than magnitude 3.5 for East-West and Far East arms race belligerents. Conflicts were listed under the date of onset and each belligerent nation in each war was rated with a single score. Correlations were then made between the six lists of war and curves A, B, and C over the time-period 1945-70. In addition a correlation was carried out between a composite of curves A, B, and C and a composite of the three large-conflicts list. The whole procedure was then repeated with the theoretical curves lagged six months in time with respect to the actual conflicts.

Here are the results:

(a) All correlations were positive and significant; hence, in the post-World War II period the onset of war is cyclic in time.

(b) Correlations for the large-conflicts lists tended to be larger than for the all-conflicts lists; therefore the onset of large wars are more predictable than small.

(c) With the exception of the Indonesian Crisis of 1965, all the large conflicts listed were at least in part international wars. Therefore, it can be concluded that arms expenditures and arms races are more related to international wars than to civil wars.

(d) The 6-month lagged curves were more highly correlated with war than the unlagged curves. This suggests that arms races lead to war more often than the reverse.

(e) The highest correlation determined was 0.53 between the lagged composite of curves A, B, and C and the composite of the three large-conflict lists. Thus much of the variance with respect to time of both arms races and war is unaccounted for.

(f) Overall, the East-West arms race seemed to predominate, for curve A correlated with warring nations all over the world. Thus, Moyal's five-year interval between the onset of war has been confirmed. Major conflict since World War II has taken place at approximately five-year intervals: 1945-46, 1950, (not 1955), 1961-62, and 1967. If the regularity continues the next peak of conflict should occur about 1972-73.

(g) Both the composite theoretical arms race curve and the composite actual onset-of-war curve peak at 1945. The theoretical curve also peaks at 1972 since all three arms races reach a maximum in 1972. 1967 is the greatest peak of the onset-of-war curve since 1945 but if predictions hold 1972-74 may be even greater. The 20-25-30 year periodicity of war found in the historical studies has been confirmed in this current study.

ALLIANCES

J. David Singer and Melvin Small (1965) undertook the investigation of the relationship of arms races to alliances. They took as their "spacial-temporal boundaries" 83 nation states over the period 1815-1945 in order to include an "appropriate mixture of stability and transition from which generalization would be legitimate." With respect to technical innovation the period "postdates the smoothbore cannon and predates the nuclear missile." With respect to political entities the period includes such historic states as Mecklenberg-Schwerin and Hesse Grand Ductal and such hardy perennials as Spain and Switzerland. War involvement, the dependent variable in their analysis was defined as any war of magnitude 3.0 or more which involved at least one of the 83 nations on both sides of the dispute. Alliance commitments, the independent variable, was defined as any written agreement, convention, or treaty which called for military intervention, neutrality, or consultation from a signatory in times of specific political or military crises. The dependent and independent variables were further refined into sub-variables such as: months of war, nation-months of war, battle deaths, alliance duration in years, type of alliance, etc., and the nations in the system were then rank-ordered according to each such variable. The resultant rank-order data were then correlated with one another giving the following results. Most correlations were positive and significant but number of alliances with a major power and number of years in the various alliances were most highly correlated with the various war indices, especially number of wars.

A second analysis was performed to investigate the association between war involvement and alliances which existed only three months before the nation's involvement in war. These correlations were highest of all, leading the researchers to conclude that "alliance commitment predicts to war involvement over the entire 131 year period, but not nearly as strongly in the nineteenth century as in the twentieth century."

(emphasis added.)

SUMMARY

There is an agreement and consistency in these different analyses of domestic and international violence which goes far beyond their occasional disagreement. Though a complete synthesis of the results will be left to Chapter 13, we can tentatively conclude that international war (and some civil war) seems to be the end product of a logical sequence with an arms race as an intermediate stage since most of the studies in this chapter point to a time sequence in their findings. Before reaching final conclusions, however, let us turn to the social science laboratory.

11 laboratory evidence---games

Social scientists, like physical or biological scientists, use two methods to obtain data: direct observation of natural events, past or present, and laboratory experiments designed to reveal unknown regularities. Astronomy, bird-watching and historical studies are examples of the direct observation technique. A characteristic of this approach is that, in general, the stars, the birds and the princes of the past are unaware or indifferent to the fact that they are being watched. On the other hand, space satellites, rat mazes and "games" are examples of laboratory experiments; the rockets, the rats and the groups of people taking part in the games have been set in motion deliberately so that their behaviour could be studied.

GAMES OF STRATEGY

"Game" theory is a relatively new science. "In the last decade and a half," Anatol Rapoport writes, "an entirely new mathematical approach to a theory of conflict has arisen, called the theory of games. The word 'game' in this context is not meant to imply a lack of seriousness but rather the idea that so-called 'parlor games,' more appropriately called 'games of strategy,' offer the purest examples of situations which are taken as prototypes in this new theory of conflict. In these situations, 'rationality' is central." (Rapoport, 1960, p. 109.)

Games of strategy offer a good model of the rational and irrational behaviour of people in situations characterized by: (1) conflicts of interest; (2) the existence of a number of alternatives open at each phase of the situation; (3) the presence of people in a position to estimate consequences of their choices, taking into consideration the important circumstance that outcomes are determined not only by their own choices but also by the choices of others, over whom they have no direct control. There are, broadly speaking, two classes of games: zero-sum and non zero-sum. In a zero-sum game, what player A wins, player B loses, and vice-versa so that the sum of the two payoffs or rewards is always zero. In a non zero-sum game, the sum of the two payoffs may be zero, less than zero or greater than zero. In the two-person, non zero-sum game nicknamed "Prisoner's Dilemma," for example, each player has two choices: he may "cooperate" with his opponent or he may "compete." Neither player knows what choice his opponent has made until both have decided, at which point each is informed of the other's decision before making the next play. Anywhere from 50 to 300 plays constitute an experiment for any pair of players, but once they have played a game they should not play again with the same set of rules. The payoffs may be as follows: if both players cooperate, each receives one point (or 1¢ or $1 as originally decided, and announced, by the experimenter). If both players compete, each loses one point. So why don't they always cooperate? Because if player A cooperates but player B competes, then B wins two points (or 2¢ or $2) while A loses two points.

The object of the game for each player is to win as much as possible for himself. And each player's dilemma is in deciding what motive to impute to his opponent—greed, rivalry, dominance, curiosity, love or altruism? It is important that he be able to predict what his opponent is likely to do. If both play "rationally" and consider the most likely effect of competitive play on their opponents, then they should always play cooperatively, for in that way each side always wins something, and together they take money from the experimenter (who presumably has a grant!). The fun and interest in the game comes when, after a brief period of cooperation (and sometimes less than brief), one side "cheats" to improve or increase his personal gains.

Another example of the non zero-sum game is a simplified model of deterrence called "Chicken." Chicken differs from Prisoner's Dilemma only when both sides play competitively; then the payoff is disastrously negative (-10, -100 or even -1,000 points for each player). All other payoffs are the same. Rapoport tells the story of two countries, Jedesland and Andersland, which both would be better off if neither attacked the other. But nonetheless some of the Jedeslanders argue that

> ... Jedesland should attack Andersland before

> the latter has the chance to do the same. When both, at last, have their missile-launchers zeroed in on each other's cities, the "necessity" to launch the attack first seems imperative. There is, however, perhaps a speck of sanity left in those who control the final irrevocable act. Yet, as they become aware of the "necessity," they cannot but become convinced that the other is probably coming to the same conclusion. The imagined "necessity" is thus self-confirming and re-affirming. The more certain it seems, the more inescapable it becomes, at an accelerating rate, ending ultimately in a mad rush on both sides to the launching platforms. "Two scorpions in a bottle," to use Robert Oppenheimer's gloomy comparison. (Rapoport, 1960, p. 178.)

Obviously communication would be of benefit to both sides if it were possible. Indeed, concludes Rapoport, "the best payoff plays a prominent part in games where communication (collusion) is allowed." Two Prisoner's Dilemma experiments, experiment A, in which collusion was allowed (Radow, 1965), and experiment B, in which it was not (Pylyshyn, 1966), demonstrate this.

In experiment A, 28 male students were briefed on the rules and payoffs of the game, which consisted of 98 plays. The students were then seated in pairs before a console with two pushbuttons and a number of coloured lights to inform each player of his opponent's choice and the sum of money which each has received as a result of this play. Rather larger sums than usual were paid out on the assumption that, "if the payments are small, the players may be more interested in competing with each other than in maximizing monetary return." Results tended to confirm this assumption, as there was more cooperative play than in similar studies previously reported. Play still was predominantly competitive, however. The average pattern of play for the 28 students followed the shape of a hammock: At the start most played cooperatively, but only 49 percent still were playing cooperatively at play 7. By play 58 the number had dropped to a low of 26% from which point cooperative play rose steadily, reaching 52 percent by play 98, the end of the game.

The second part of experiment A involved another 24 male students. In addition to the instructions given in experiment A, the second group of students received supplemental instructions deliberately designed to encourage collusion by forcing the players to consider how their actions would be viewed by their experimental partners. Here, in part, is what they were told: It should be clear to you that you can cooperate in dividing the $8 payment, or you can compete for a larger share of a smaller amount. This should be understood clearly and you should decide on your strategy now, for if you decide on one strategy now and decide to change it later, you will find it difficult to convince the other player that you will stick to the new strategy. You should also know that previous subjects in this experiment have done about anything it is possible to do. Some have pressed the left button all the time. Some have pressed the right button all the time. And some have pressed various mixtures of right and left buttons. Feel free to select any series of choices that you feel are in your interest.

The instructor may simply have explained the game more clearly, he may have influenced the student players more than he thought, or a collusion process may have taken place, such that the two players "ganged up" on the instructor to extract more money from him. In any case, the results were dramatic, for "in spite of the apparent neutrality of the more comprehensive instructions, the players (in part II) were predominantly cooperative in their choices." No fewer than 73 percent chose cooperative moves by play 7. Dropping to 54 percent by play 63, cooperation rose to 81 percent by play 98. Though a mixture of the two strategies was still the general rule, this high proportion of cooperative plays is strong evidence for the value of communication.

In the second experiment with Prisoner's Dilemma (experiment B), one player was both an intensely rational man and a living example of nonviolence. For him, even without special instructions, it was quite natural to choose the cooperative strategy, for he saw that in the long run both sides stood to gain more that way. If either subject chose to increase his short-term gain he would alienate his opponent who would become competitive, even though he may originally have played cooperatively. And, of course, if either side played competitively at all, the sum of the payoff for the two players would always be less than if both played the cooperative game.

So the "rational" player operated the buttons cooperatively not once, not twice, but persistently. With what result? His opponent, seeing an immediate—and possibly short-term—advantage in playing competitively, persistently did so. The rational player did not change his strategy; "surely," he reasoned, "my opponent will see that it is to our mutual long-term advantage to cooperate." His opponent never "learned" but continued to win the largest possible reward, for he saw only that he had, for some unknown reason, a cooperating "sucker" for an opponent. (And who was he to question the long-term gain, when the short-term payoff was so good?) For the "sucker," the rational believer in nonviolence, the experience was traumatic.

Is this an extreme case? Yes, to the extent that one participant would spontaneously be a sucker (or saint) for so long. Rapoport reports that to his knowledge 72 cooperative moves in a row is the longest example of unbroken cooperation on record. (Rapoport, 1967, p. 15.)

It is not an extreme case, however, with respect to the reaction of the opponent. When a "stooge" (a player in league with the experimenter) was instructed to take the saint role, more than 50 percent of all opponents took the exploitative role, that is, played competitively throughout.

According to results reported by Kenneth Terhune, (Terhune, 1966) exploitation is heightened if the personality characteristic of the opponent is of the authoritarian type. In his experiment, Terhune separated 148 male undergraduate students into three groups: people motivated primarily by a need for achievement (desire to meet a standard of excellence), by a need for affiliation (desire to maintain friendly relations with others) and by a need for power (desire to exert control over others). The personality types were determined by means of a

"Thematic Aperception Test" in which subjects were required to write stories about six ambiguous pictures shown to them for the purpose. Nine trained coders scored the tests.

Matched pairs (e.g., both high-scoring Achievers) then played three one-shot Prisoner's Dilemma games; that is, they made three competitive or cooperative choices without feedback from their opponent. This, reasoned Terhune, allowed a "pure" decision to be made, unaffected by the opponent's decision. To test the effect of temptation or threat, he raised the penalty for defection over the three trials. The matched pairs of players were given neutral instructions: "How much you gain will depend on what you do and what the other person does. Your success in earning money will be affected by the tactics you adopt."

Terhune hypothesized that the Affiliation subjects would play mainly cooperatively, the Power subjects would play mainly competitively and the Achievers would mix the two strategies. As expected, he found that the Power subjects played competitively. Subjects with a need for achievement, however, played more cooperatively, while the Affiliators played a mixed strategy.

When recording their three choices, players were asked to indicate what they thought their opponents would do. The Achievers, who played more cooperatively themselves, expected cooperation from their opponents; the Power-oriented players, who most consistently played competitively, nevertheless expected cooperation (they were apparently playing their opponent for a sucker to maximize their own gains); and the Affiliators, who played a mixture of cooperation and competition, expected defection from their opponents. Whether hopeful or defensive, in either case they were suspicious of their opponents.

The results of this Prisoner's Dilemma experiment tie in with the personality and ideology attitude studies reported in Chapter 8 and are consistent with the following alignment: the Achiever falls somewhere in the lower left quadrant (See Figure 4, p. 114) likely close to the horizontal axis (Terhune concludes that they must be guided by "enlightened self-interest"). The Affiliators (whom he calls "defensive or lacking in trust") are close to the horizontal axis of the upper right quadrant (Irresponsibility); while those with a desire for power clearly fall close to the vertical axis of the upper right quadrant (Punitiveness).

It is important to realize that Terhune's study indicates that attitude studies measure more than attitude, for these games are a measure of action. Apparently, given the facilities to act on their bent, players do tend to follow their personalities. Terhune concludes: "Results show Achievers to be more cooperative, Affiliators to be most defensive and hence conflictual, and those with a desire for Power the most exploitative and hence conflictual.... But as either temptation or perception of threat increased, differences among the motive groups tended to disappear." (Terhune, 1968.)

This type of experiment suggests that in the real world, as opposed to the game world, military or industrial leaders, in fact, bureaucratic leaders in general, would exploit the weakness of an opponent if they could get away with it. In international relations, it suggests that unilateral disarmament, or "turning the other cheek," would be likely to invite prompt invasion.

SIMULATION

Are games of strategy relevant to the flesh-and-blood conflicts of the real world? It must be admitted that they do have the following basic weaknesses:

(1) A set of alternatives is presented to the player, and on the basis of rewards known to him he is asked to plan a strategy or series of moves which will bring him the best reward, although he is uncertain of what his opponent will do. But in the real world situation the player, or decision-maker, faces not only uncertainty as to his opponent's actions but, as noted by Kenneth Boulding in Conflict and Defence, he faces uncertainty as to the payoffs themselves. (Boulding, 1961, p. 57.)

(2) Games of strategy are supposedly based on deliberate rational choice, or on what a decision-maker would do if he stopped to think. This assumption is directly contrary to the assumption used by Lewis Richardson in his analysis of international behaviour. He believed that the most appropriate model of international behaviour was one in which the leaders act irrationally, that is, did not stop to think. Certainly history has had its rational leaders; but can anyone doubt than an element of irrationality crept into Germany's war preparations before World War I when the Kaiser was reputedly goaded by the thought, "I must have a Navy as good as Grandmama's." (Russell, 1952, p. 133.)

Games of strategy thus are gravely limited in their

application to foreign affairs. On the positive side, however, is that what the games lose in "realism" they gain in scientific rigour, for the "statistics" of the same simple game played over and over are excellent.

In an effort to achieve greater realism without sacrificing scientific validity, more elaborate games which "simulate" international behaviour have been developed during the past 15 years and used with increasing frequency. (Guetzkow and Jensen, 1966.) One model, known as inter-nation simulation, or INS for short, stems largely from the pioneering work of Harold Guetzkow and his colleagues at Northwestern University. Like games of strategy, simulation offers to the researcher explicitness, experimental control and an opportunity for replication. With the exception of all-computer INS simulation, however, the experimental conditions are not nearly so precise as in games theory. Partly this is because the payoffs in simulation are less accurately known; partly it is due to poorer immediate communication and to a more complicated and flexible set of rules. But for these reasons, INS simulation reflects the real world more closely than limited-choice games like Prisoner's Dilemma or Chicken.

Internation simulation is based on three principles; that nations do not act in isolation but, on the contrary, continuously interact with each other; that the policy decisions of a nation generally are made by a small group of leaders; and that these decision-makers are influenced by various national factors, such as the state of the economy and the demands of their citizens. To duplicate or simulate the international situation, INS uses live decision-makers (students, professors and government officials, for example), who act out leadership roles according to a set of rules. Along with the rules is a set of calculations which represents the influences or constraints imposed upon the decision-makers as a result of actions which they themselves have made; these factors are different for each country involved. Although the actors must adhere to the rules of the game, they are allowed great freedom to arrange conferences, organize aid and trade with other countries, plan military strategies, organize alliances, etc.

Usually an INS consists of five to 10 nations with three or four players representing each nation (premier, finance minister, defence minister and foreign secretary), plus an international organization (a simulated United Nations) to represent the world. Time is compressed in the experiment so that 2 hours of play may represent 3 months or even a year in the real world.

To lend realism and to simulate the key role of the communication media, a "world newspaper" is published frequently and sometimes a closed-circuit world radio or TV station makes regular broadcasts. "Runs" with any given group of participants last from 2 to 3 days. For one experiment, 10 to 20 runs based on the same model usually are made.

Background information, with or without ideological bias built in, is provided through condensed histories of each country given to each participant before the run begins. The key factors which in part guide his actions during play are listed on a decision form which, with the aid of computer calculations, is amended each period by the experimental staff. Through these decision forms players learn the positive or negative results of allocations made by them in the previous period. At the end of each period they are required to divide the output of their "basic resources" (factories and farms) between consumer goods (butter and boots), military defence (men and material) and research and development (to increase their productivity rates). Moreover, the players are given ratings from 1 to 10 for "consumer satisfaction," "national security satisfaction" and sometimes "international opinion satisfaction" and the "decision latitude" which they will be allowed in the next period. Careful attention must be paid to these four variables, which result from their own and the other teams' actions, for they determine whether the nations's leader will stay in office (a strong motivation) and whether his country is likely to have an election upset or a revolution. These abstractions can become so meaningful, together with the human interaction of meetings, messages and news reports, that players frequently feel intense emotional involvement to the point of acute discomfort. In one run, a Danish player ordered a nuclear attack and then fainted dead away. (Laulicht, 1966.)

Two recent simulation studies illustrate the versatility and power of INS. Though they have been reported separately, Richard Brody's analysis of the "nth Country Problem" (Brody, 1963) and J. R. Raser and W. J. Crow's analysis of the "Invulnerable Deterrent" (Raser and Crow, 1966) are worth assessing together. Both studies deal with the effect on national posture when a nation substantially increases its weapon power. More significantly, both deal with the effect on other countries of this increase in weapon power.

Raser and Crow simulate the interaction between five countries, three in one bloc, two in another bloc; Brody's study is of seven nations, split four to three. In both cases, each bloc is led by a powerful nation, which has a monopoly on nuclear weapons. The Raser and Crow study is concerned with what happens when one of these bloc leaders acquires an invulnerable deterrent; i.e., when, through hardened missile sites and a civil defence program, it has the capacity to absorb a nuclear attack and then, deliberately and in its own time, to mount a retaliatory attack. Brody is interested in the interaction between all seven nations of his simulated world when one by one they all "go nuclear." His experiment anticipates changes in the relationship between blocs and among nations within a bloc.

The techniques used by the experimenters to measure results differ in some respects. Both rely to some extent on direct evaluations which participants are required to make of each other from time to time concerning hostility, trustworthiness, helpfulness, danger to world peace, etc. But in addition to these ratings, Brody and his colleagues devised an elaborate information retrieval system built on the 9,000-odd messages which passed between participants during the 17 three-day runs which made up their experiment (Raser and Crow used 12 runs of three days each). Based on their content, the messages were classified by two experimenters into one of eight compass point divisions to reflect their position on a friendship-hostility continuum (North-South) and on a dominance-submission continuum (East-West). In addition they were given a single or double rating as a measure of the intensity of feeling which the content conveyed.

The two studies measured two different military strategies. In the first only one nation altered its strategy and power while in the second all the weaker nations increased their strength. Nevertheless, results from these two disparate experiments were strikingly similar.

In the Raser and Crow study, the United States (called OMNE) felt stronger when she had achieved an invulnerable deterrent; by the same token, when she subsequently lost it, the Soviet Union (called UTRO) felt stronger. OMNE's allies perceived her as stronger with "invulnerability," weaker without it. With her greater strength OMNE also was considered a greater threat to peace by her enemies. But not only was she considered a greater threat, she was a greater threat: A total of 21 military attacks occurred during the 72 periods when OMNE had "invulnerability" (13 of them launched by OMNE), compared to only seven attacks (three launched by OMNE) during the 72 periods when she was vulnerable. Moreover, her enemies not only considered her more threatening, they also acknowledged that they felt more deterred when she had "second-strike" capability; that is, the capability of retaliation after suffering a nuclear attack.

As each country in Brody's nth country experiment succeeded in becoming a nuclear nation, it considered enemy nations as less threatening. Moreover, nations within the same bloc considered an ally more threatening once it had "gone nuclear" even though they may have in the meantime developed nuclear weapons themselves. Not surprisingly, enemy nations were always perceived as more hostile (able to do harm) than allies. Content analysis of the various messages between nations revealed that each nation became more hostile to other nations once it acquired nuclear weapons. In addition, some interesting dependent relationships were shown to exist within the blocs. Before the spread of nuclear weapons, the two major powers acted as communication centers for their respective blocs and as the communication agents for messages between blocs; also, the volume of messages within blocs was greater than between blocs. As Brody says, "The system was comprised of two hierarchical, cohesive, bloc-alliances." (Brody, 1963.) But after proliferation, the flow of messages between nations of opposing blocs tended to be the same as between nations within a bloc; moreover, messages to the enemy leader were as frequent as to the friendly leader. Nevertheless, members of blocs did not disassociate themselves completely after nuclear spread, for a hierarchy structure still remained within each. Apparently "dependency on the bloc leader and the hierarchical ordering of the bloc stem from both military and economic insufficiencies and the economic insufficiencies continued into the post spread (nuclear proliferation) situation." (Brody, 1963.)

The results from these two independent studies seem to show that:

(1) An imbalance in weapons between enemy blocs

favours the stronger side which feels stronger, is considered stronger and is therefore more feared by the enemy bloc. The weaker bloc is thus more effectively deterred, but the stronger is more likely to engage in war deliberately.

(2) An imbalance in weapons within an alliance causes the weaker nations to be dominated by the stronger power. With greater equality in weapons, this dominance is diminished although significant influence is retained by the stronger power if there remains a large economic differential between nations in the bloc.

Simulation can thus test out policies and their implementation's likely effect in the real world. Moreover, the effect of that implementation on the participants themselves can also be determined. (Druckman, 1968.) When the subjects taking part in the Crow and Raser study—naval recruits who had been assigned randomly to their roles and nations—were asked in a carefully disguised questionnaire to assess the personalities of their fellow players, a surprising thing happened. Their 5-day-fashioned nationalism revealed itself in a characteristic bias. Players on the average gave more favourable ratings to their own nation's members, followed by allies and enemies in that order. Strong enemies were "respected" more, but weak enemies were better "liked." When alliances shifted in the course of some runs, the personality ratings shifted correspondingly. If "nationalism" can be so indoctrinated in the course of a five-day game, small wonder that it is such a potent force in shaping one's aggression over the course of a 60-year life.

It may be argued that these are just exercises, far

removed from reality, which show only one thing—how 357 high school students or enlisted navy men will react when playing a game. No one will more readily admit that simulation has not yet been adequately "validated" (that is, tested against reality) than those who developed the technique. Conscious of its many possible limitations, or indeed systematic errors, they have diligently sought to improve the model so that it may one day accurately predict the actions and reactions between countries. It is therefore notable that, in an attempt to validate these results, correspondence was found between the Stanford University World War I data and nine of the 13 hypotheses of the Brody study. (Guetzkow and Jensen, 1966.)

12 the causes of war

In writing the previous chapters we have been not unlike the four blind men suddenly confronted by an elephant: each one of them described only the part of the animal he touched—the trunk, tusk, tail or leathery wall of flesh. It is now time for us to join our disparate views into a composite picture of war.

The evidence presented so far, however, suffers from a severe limitation which must affect any attempt to construct an adequate theory of war. At the present stage of development of the social sciences—whether cultural anthropology, political science, economics, social psychology, sociology, or geography—it is easier to prove a "correlation" than a rigid law. In other words, a number of different variables can be found which affect each other, more or less, but no group of variables is so complete that it can be shown to "control" all the others. How much different it is from physical science! The social scientist, with his present precision of measurement and control of the variables concerned, would say of Ohm's Law that electrical current and voltage have a high positive correlation with resistance, while the physicist can categorically say R equals E over I. If social scientists had to invent an atomic bomb, with their present degree of precision and control of the variables concerned, they would have to base it on an equation where E correlates with m—their equation would not even have a c, much less a c^2. It is possible that war will someday be explained by a complex Ohm's Law, a set of laws like Maxwell's equations or, more probably, since we are dealing with humans, a dynamic statistical theory like that used by meteorologists. If so, what variables would be essential?

INNATE DRIVES

Konrad Lorenz (Chapter 3, page 19) spoke of four main drives which dominated the animal world: feeding, reproduction, flight and aggression (aggression was defined as "the fighting instinct in beast and man which is directed against members of the same species"). Lorenz recognized, however, a whole "parliament" or lesser instincts which could combine or compete with the big four. Among these lesser drives was a bond which keeps certain individuals together for life. This bond, wrote Lorenz, "is analogous with those human functions that go hand in hand with the emotions of love and friendship in their purest and noblest form." (Lorenz, 1966.)

In 1915 Sigmund Freud wrote of two groups of primal instincts: the <u>self-preservation</u> or ego instinct and the <u>species preservation</u> or sexual instinct. He noted, however, that "It is always possible that an exhaustive study of the other neurotic affections may oblige us to make a different classification of the primal instincts." (Freud, 1915, p. 67.) By 1932 he had indeed altered his classifications and wrote of two kinds of instincts, "those which seek to preserve and unite—which we call 'erotic'—and those which seek to destroy and kill and which we class together as the aggressive or destructive instinct." (Freud, 1932, p. 280.) They are, he said, the "universally familiar opposites between Love and Hate." Neither instinct is any less essential than the other, Freud maintained, for though love would seem to be the more constructive instinct, conflicts of interest are settled by the use of violence. "This is true (that conflicts are settled by violence) of the whole animal kingdom, from which men have no business to exclude themselves." (Freud, 1932, p. 274.)

Bertrand Russell has stated that "all human activity is prompted by desire or impulse." Those desires which are politically important may be divided into a primary and a secondary group. "In the primary group come the necessities of life: food and shelter and clothing.... In the secondary group are four in particular which we can label acquisitiveness, rivalry, vanity and love of power." (Russell, 1952, p. 134.) Acquisitiveness is less strong than rivalry, but "great as is the influence of the motives we have been considering, there is one which outweighs them all, I mean the love of power." (Russell, 1952, p. 134.) Love of power is closely akin to vanity, according to Russell. Moreover, "a man who is actuated by love of power is more apt to inflict pain than to permit pleasure." (Russell, 1952, p. 134.)

Russell recognized other drives which, though less

fundamental politically, are still of considerable importance. Love of excitement is one. Two others, which are interwoven with many other political motives, are the closely related passions of fear and hate. "It is normal to hate what we fear, and it happens frequently that we fear what we hate ... an alien herd will be avoided or fought according to our circumstances. It is this primitive mechanism which still controls our instinctive reaction to foreign nations." (Russell, 1952, p. 139.)

"I do not deny that altruistic motives exist," wrote Russell. "Sympathy is a genuine motive.... Men have been capable of love, of sympathy for the whole human race." (1952, p. 141.)

ATTITUDES

For convenience, let us try to relate the four main drives of Lorenz, the two primal instincts of Freud, the basic desires of Russell, to the war/peace attitudes measured by Eckhardt. Such a superposition is shown in Figure 6 where Eckhardt's _Punitive_ and _Responsibility_ axes are relabelled _behaviour tending to hinder the welfare of others_ and _behaviour tending to further the welfare of oneself_. Eckhardt's _Compulsion-Compassion_ axis then becomes _behaviour tending to hinder the welfare of others and oneself_ versus _behaviour tending to further the welfare of others and oneself_.

Descriptively, relationships between the various points of view are not hard to find. Russell's vanity, acquisitiveness and love of excitement are suggested by such items in the Eckhardt questionnaire as: "I like very much to keep up a good appearance; I like to own things; when I get bored I like to stir up some excitement." They are all located in his Punitive quadrant, as is "At times I feel like picking a fist fight with someone," which suggests Lorenz' definition of aggression. Alfred Adler, on the other hand has defined aggression as "any manifestation of the will to power," (English and English, 1958) which suggests a link between Russell's love of power and Lorenz' aggression.

Nervousness, anxiety and neuroticism are all located in Eckhardt's Irresponsibility quadrant and all are indications of fear, or flight as Lorenz would put it. An expression of altruism is found in such Eckhardt items as: "We should give more foreign aid to those countries which need it; The aim of the churches should be to bring out altruism;" and these are found in his Permissiveness quadrant. It is less obvious why Freud's species preservation or Lorenz' reproduction instinct would be there and yet that is where Eckhardt's sexual permissiveness items are located. Eckhardt's responsibility items relate to confidence, curiosity and the nurturing of self, in short are descriptive of ego strength; thus the positioning of the equivalent items from Russell and Freud would seem to be appropriate.

Located in the upper diagonal quadrant of Figure 6 are Russell's hate, Freud's aggressive or destructive instinct and Eckhardt's tertiary factor of compulsion. Is hate a mixture of fear and aggression, of wanting to hinder both others and oneself? The evidence suggests that it is, for the three "hate" scales of the attitude study (misanthropy, denunciation, hostility) fall on this diagonal dimension. In the bottom diagonal quadrant of Figure 6 are located Russell's sympathy for the whole human race, Freud's preserving and uniting (erotic) instinct and his love, and Lorenz' love and friendship. Is love then a mixture of self-interest and altruism, of ego and sex, or wanting to further the welfare of others and oneself? Erich Fromm has argued that it is: "love for and understanding of one's own self cannot be separated from respect and love and understanding for another individual. The love for my own self is inseparably connected with the love for any other being." (1956, p. 49.)

The attitude studies suggest that the vertical and horizontal axes of Figure 6 are the limits of a behaviour pattern which in general falls along the diagonal compulsion-compassion axis (See Figure 4.) Moreover, since we are dealing with primitive passions, each end of this pattern of social behaviour must have had great survival value for the species in the past. To what extent is this true today? And if conditions have changed, to what extent can our behaviour alter to accommodate that fact? Certainly Neanderthal man had need of fear and aggression, as he had of love and friendship. The power of his weapons were no threat to the existence of his species. However, this is no longer true today for our weapons systems have grown out of proportion. Thus man must alter his behaviour towards the compassionate end of the spectrum if his species is to survive. How this might be done is suggested by the attitude studies.

Five scales of childhood discipline consistently

Figure 6

SOCIAL BEHAVIOUR OF MAN AND OTHER ANIMALS

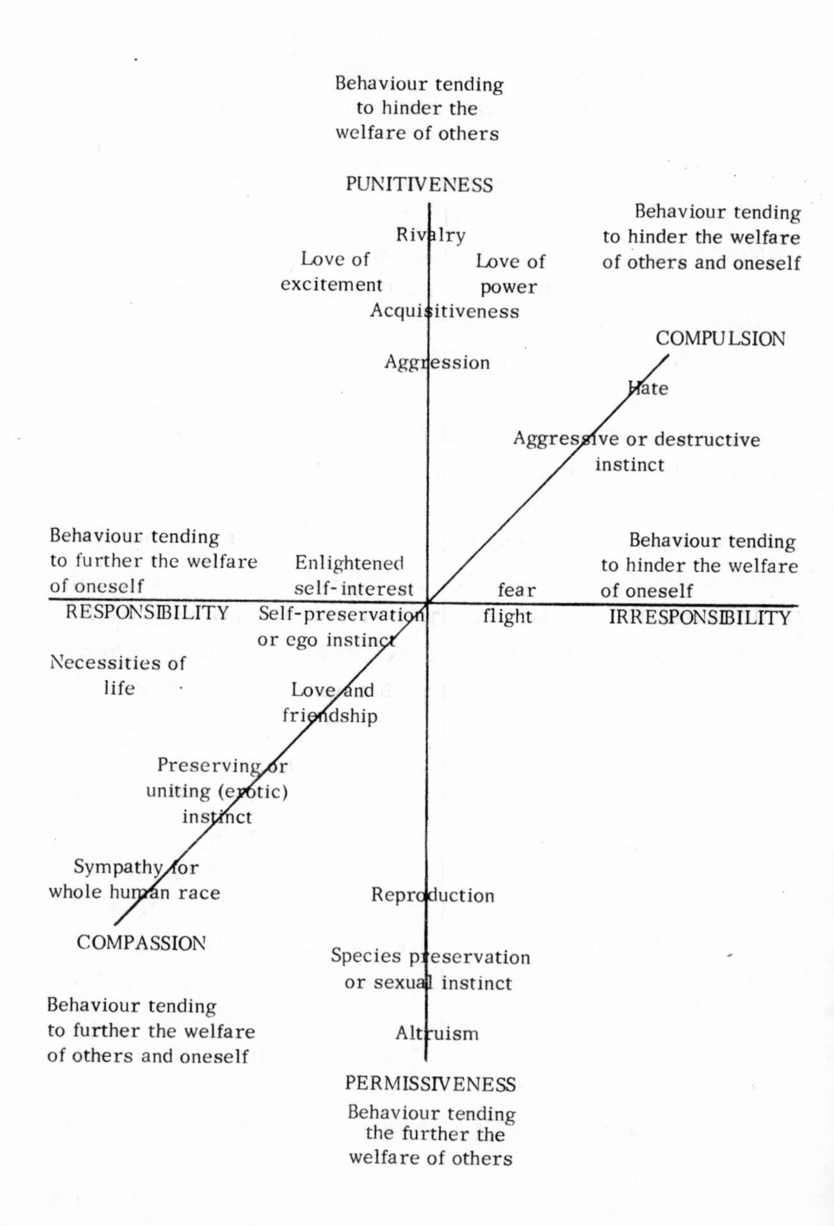

align themselves towards the compulsive end. In two ways children seem to be restricted or frustrated, giving rise to slightly different results. Whereas the "You don't do that" of normal discipline results in hostility turned inwards and ultimate feelings of insecurity (horizontal axis), the "we don't do that" of conformity turns the resultant hostility outward towards socially disapproved out-groups—Negroes, atheists, Jews and communists (the vertical axis). In both cases aggression is displaced from the source of the frustration, parent or teacher, who after all has the power to strike back. Conversely, childhood discipline in the form of praise and support is associated with security (horizontal axis), while rationality and permissiveness, including sexual permissiveness, lies along the lower end of the vertical axis. Together, the latter two forms of upbringing tend to shift a person towards the compassionate end of the spectrum, the area where all the peace attitudes lie. This analysis indicates that while human beings have the innate capacity for both hate and love, nationalism and internationalism, religious and political tolerance or intolerance, punitiveness or permissiveness, childhood training largely determines which will be dominant. As the pioneer ethologist Nikolaas Tinbergen put it: "human aggression results from the cultural reinforcement of a biological heritage that man shares with the animals." (Genovés, 1970, p. 74.)

IDEOLOGIES

In the attitude studies, nationalism, conservatism,

and religiosity are more or less consistently linked with a disposition to war (militarism)—especially in the West. Does history bear out this association? In order to test out this hypothesis we have rearranged Richardson's data. In Table 14 his 429 pairs of belligerents are grouped to show the extent of differences in nationality, religion, class or political ideology in both foreign and civil wars. Participants in civil war have been subdivided into pairs of belligerents who were either indigenous to different parts of the country (as in the American Civil War) or who had intermingled on the same territory prior to the war (as in the First Chinese Communist War of 1927). (The columns total more than 100 percent because the various characteristics overlap, i.e., belligerents of different nationalities also can be of a different class or religion.)

Under religion Richardson included not only Christianity, Taoism, Mohammedanism, etc., but also communism; in this altered tabulation, communism is listed under political ideology. The following items from Richardson's classification were included in the last two columns: indicating class, "one group habitually orders the other group to obey" and "one group was evidently richer than the other"; indicating political ideology, "monarchists versus liberals or moderates, democrats versus fascists, communists versus fascists" and "one group believed in a greater degree of personal liberty than the other" (for example, the American Civil War).

From the data used for Table 14 it was also determined that:

(1) At least one ideological difference—national,

Table 14

IDEOLOGICAL DIFFERENCES VERSUS TYPE OF WAR

(pairs of belligerents in all wars of magnitude 3.5 to 7.5 from 1820-1945)

Type of War	Ideological Difference								Total number of pairs
	Nationality		Religion		Class		Political Ideology		
	number	%	number	%	number	%	number	%	
Foreign	297	100	131	44	12	4	0	0	297
Civil (different territory)	48	50	38	40	34	35	16	16	96
Civil (same territory)	2	6	16	44	18	50	13	36	36

religious, class, or political—existed between all pairs of belligerents, except two: the Turkish Janissaries versus the Turkish Regular Army and the Clan Satsuma versus the Japanese Army.

(2) Territorial differences existed between all pairs of belligerents, except the 36 pairs of civil war belligerents who had intermingled on the same territory before the war.

(3) Of these 36 pairs, 18 were of different classes; of the remainder, 10 were of different political ideology and two were of different nationality.

(4) The six pairs remaining are accounted for by three massacres: the Armenians versus the Kurds in 1894, the Armenians versus the Turks in 1909, and the Jews versus the Germans, Vichy French, Fascist Rumanians, and Anti-Communist Hungarians in 1939. In each case there was a difference of religion between belligerents.

Thus, a common factor in conflict, according to Richardson's data, is some difference in ideology. Of 429 pairs of belligerents, only two did not conform to this rule, and it is worth noting by way of possible explanation that both the Janissaries and the Samurai (who fought in the Satsuma Rebellion) were rigid, almost fanatical, elite groups of professional soldiers.

But a difference in ideology is not the only difference between the pairs of belligerents in Table 14. All but 36 of the pairs of belligerents (92 percent) occupied different territories before the war; that is, they lived on different sides of a territorial boundary (see Chapters 3 and 5 for the importance of boundaries). One might be tempted to conclude that a territorial difference as well as an ideological difference is a vital factor in precipitating war, but this argument, again, is weakened by the fact that not all belligerents satisfied the criterion. It is strengthened, however, to the extent that one can interpret a political or class difference (but not a religious difference) as a difference over the control of land. In this sense, 98 percent of all belligerents might be said to have had "a territorial difference." But because political or class differences can involve control of the means of production as well as control of land, further research is certainly required.

The 2 percent residue of quarrels includes the Armenian and Jewish massacres, to which no territorial disputes seem to pertain. A possible explanation is that these special cases are examples of a "displacement" effect; i.e., an indigenous group served as a scapegoat for thwarted external aggression. It is a subject worthy of research.

The historical studies reveal that differences in ideology cause tensions; the attitude studies suggest which ideologies are most likely to contribute to these tensions.

Nationalism

Historically, Spanish-speaking people were more warlike than those speaking Chinese. According to the cross-cultural survey nationalism in all six continents was positively correlated with militarism; indeed no other attitude was so consistently linked with a disposition towards war. Thus, either Spanish nationalists and Chinese nationalists are both militarists, but in differing degrees, or some other characteristic—like language or religion—is the distinguishing variable.

Political Ideology

In the cross-cultural survey, capitalism (part of the conservatism cluster) has been identified in all continents but one (Africa) with the punitive factor, that is, it is linked directly with militarism and/or nationalism. Moreover, the military nature of capitalism was confirmed in another survey, where leading Canadian businessmen were more in favour of nuclear weapons than any other elite group, and were more in favour of conventional weapons and more opposed to the United Nations than any other group including the general public.

Religion

Of all ideological attitudes, religion presents the most confused picture. Historically, Richardson found that Christians versus Moslems were an uncommonly belligerent combination. Currently, religiosity in the West (which means Christianity) is consistently linked with militarism. But in Africa, Christianity is independent of militarism. And in Asia, religiosity (which means Buddhism and Hinduism) is negatively correlated with militarism. Who and where is the God of love? An answer to this question has been proposed by psychologist Elbert W. Russell (1971). He distinguishes between conditional and unconditional love. Judaism, Christianity and Mohammedanism are the militaristic religions, being based on the conditional love of the Old Testament. Buddhism, Hinduism and Taoism, and a few small sects or outgrowths of Christianity (Anabaptists, Quakers, Unitarians) are not militaristic religions, since they emphasize unconditional love. Christians will maintain that their inspiration is the _unconditional_ love of

Jesus (for example: "Father, forgive them; for they know not what they do." Luke 23:34.) Russell shows, by means of a content analysis of the New Testament, that most of Christ's sayings, as reported in the four gospels, illustrate conditional love ("And these shall go away into everlasting punishment: but the righteous into life eternal." Matthew 25:46.) Russell's interpretation is consistent with the facts though Africa remains anomalous. A possible explanation for Africa is the newly reported discovery (Eckhardt, 1971) that Christianity is not linked with militarism for children. Perhaps both Sunday schools and mission schools teach unconditional love. But Christian churches teach conditional love. The mystery of the Spanish-speaking people versus the Chinese-speaking people seems to be cleared up—the operative factor _is_ religion.

Class

Table 14 (which lists foreign and civil wars separately) suggests that class conflict is of little consequence in international struggles but is a factor in 35 percent of civil conflicts if the belligerents are from different territories, and 50 percent if they share the same territitory. Clearly class differences are related to war and the Marx-Lenin interpretation of history is at least partially correct. Indeed, together with the above indictments of capitalism and religion, the case is especially strong. Marx' grasp of man's institutions was immense. Had he understood as clearly the role of man's natural drives—his urge for territory and its manifestation in nationalism today—Marx' views of war would have required little modification.

Race and Language

Race and language have been left to the last because of their minimum relationship to war (see Richardson and Rokeach). In a secondary way both are important, for both serve as indicators of class. From the analysis of capitalism it is clear that the upper class is implicated because of its power, not because of its colour or language.

13 a dynamic theory of war

The previous pages have isolated a number of key variables essential to an understanding of war. Before linking them into a dynamic theory of war—that is, the actual forces which set war into motion—it seems instructive to consolidate them into a number of propositions.

These propositions are based on data from earlier chapters. Most of the propositions cannot be labelled as scientific facts; they are simply propositions—statements put forward as true, or as something to be tested for truth. The propositions which follow are tentative, but they are nevertheless based on the best scientific evidence available today.

ELEMENTS OF WAR

Aggression, defined as an urge to fight other members of the same species, is an independent instinct in animals.

Aggression is an innate tendency in man.

Defence of territory, by means of aggression, is

an instinct in animals.

Defence of territory, by means of aggression, is a widespread tendency in primitive societies of man.

Defence of territory, by means of aggression, is a widespread tendency in advanced societies of man.

Aggression tends to occur over territorial boundaries for animals.

Aggression tends to occur over territorial boundaries for man.

The greater an animal's power (within a given species), the greater his territory.

The greater the power of the weapons of a primitive society of man, the greater its territory.

The threshold for aggression is lowered by social crowding in animals.

The threshold for aggression is lowered by social crowding (urban stress) in man.

Aggression is decreased by fear, an independent instinct in animals.

Fear increases with distance from home in animals.

Aggression decreases with distance from home for advanced societies of man.

Leaders of animal groups determine in large part how aggressive the group will be.

Authoritarianism causes an advanced society of man to be more aggressive.

Leaders of animal groups usually identify the foe

for the younger members.
Leaders of groups of men usually identify the foe.

Foes and friends for an animal are distinguished by differences or similarities of smell, sight, sound, or behaviour.
Foes and friends for man are distinguished by differences or similarities of national, religious, class, and political belief systems.

If the underlined elements of these propositions are linked together as succinctly as possible, the validity of the linkage can be tested by considering the dynamics of the system: how in practice each verbal element or action affects the others.

War is an overt action resulting from man's innate aggressiveness. Like other social animals, groups of men defend their home territories at definite boundaries and aggressively seek to own or control larger territories in keeping with the aggressiveness and fear of their leaders and the power of their weapons and those of their friends compared to those of their foes. Friends and foes are identified by the leaders by means of similarities or differences of national culture, religion, class, or political ideology. Aggression is increased by social stress and by authoritarianism, and decreased by distance of a disputed territory from home.

Let us now consider how these 20 elements of war interact with one another.

DYNAMICS OF WAR

"Arms races are not made by reason and knowledge, but by instinct and suspicion," wrote Richardson. He ignored reason except as implicit in the various constants of his equations, and reason will also be ignored in the following analysis of the dynamics of the war system unless it is necessary to account for the facts.

The Richardson equations may not exactly describe the dynamic process underlying an arms race or war. They are, nevertheless, consistent with two arms build-ups—World Wars I and II—and consistent with the build-up of casualties of at least one shooting war—Vietnam. Of equal importance, if the Richardson equations are suitably relabelled, they can also describe the primitive reactions between two competing members of a species, man or animal. Recall (see page 71) that the rate of change of an arms build-up was accounted for by three terms: (1) grievance or ambition (2) a positive term representing the menace of the enemy (3) a negative term representing the fatigue of maintaining armaments. Now for ambition, substitute dominance or territorial ambition. For menace of the enemy, substitute aggressiveness towards a competitor of one's own species. For fatigue, substitute fear of the competitor. For arms expenditures of either side (a measure of power) substitute distance from home of either side (also a measure of power). Then the arms races of modern nations and the thrust and parry of fighting fish are described by the same equations. Fear increases for a fighting fish with distance from home; aggression increases for a fish when a foe nears his home. It has been found that fighting fish always oscillate towards a stable point at the boundary between their two territories (see page 21). If either fish alters his dominance or ambition—upwards by taking on a mate who shares his fighting role, or downwards by raising young and thereby losing her assistance—his territory immediately grows or shrinks proportionately, for the boundary is constantly challenged and shifts according to the balance of power.

There are, however, two subtle distinctions between fish and human nations. First, though fish invariably reach a stable point, arms races are not always stable. This distinction is more apparent than real. In actual fact, distance from home for two competing fish cannot increase indefinitely, for neither can be greater than the distance between the two nests. But the armament expenditures of two nations cannot increase indefinitely either, for they are limited ultimately by their Gross National Products. Thus as either distance or armaments increase, a stable point is reached. This is equivalent to saying that near the boundary point rivalry becomes the prevailing condition, and as we have seen (page 73) rivalry always reaches a point a stability.

The second subtle distinction between fish and human nations is real, not merely apparent. While fish immediately alter their boundaries as their fighting power changes, nations only alter their fighting power. Their boundaries remain fixed, for an arms race isn't a war. Thus, the Richardson equations simultaneously describe shifts in the power <u>and</u> territory is an exact measure of power; but they only describe shifts in power between nations of men.

describe shifts in power between nations of men.

The situation has been precisely stated by Kenneth Boulding in Conflict and Defense, a book which stands as a unique reference work in the theory of conflict:

> During peace, that is, international conflict by diplomacy, it is impossible to make any but the most minor and insignificant adjustment in international boundaries. Because of the slowly changing relative power of nations, however, the existing structure of boundaries gets more and more obsolete and is subject to greater and greater strain. Eventually, the strain gets too great for the system of diplomacy and war breaks out. War creates a fluidity in national boundaries that did not exist under diplomacy.... In the treaty that follows the war, a new set of boundaries is drawn, presumably corresponding more than the old set to the structure of national power that the war has revealed. The strain on the national system is thereby reduced, and diplomacy is once more feasible as an international system" (Boulding, 1961, p. 264.)

LEADERSHIP

But whether a nation will actually go to war to alter its boundaries (or a partisan group will revolt to control its land) is another question, for the act of going to war is, in general, separate from the dynamics of an arms race. Or is it? Richardson said his equations describe what a nation would do, "if it did not stop to think." The launching of war, however, has generally been thought of as a deliberate act with some degree of human volition.

Though Richardson applied his equations to nations, the role of their leaders was very much in his thoughts; in Arms and Insecurity (Richardson, 1960[b], p. 231) he wrote:

> Critic: In view of the evidence at the Nüremberg Trial I suppose that you will now admit that Hitler and his associates planned the war deliberately.
>
> Author: Yes, the evidence of formerly secret documents convinces me of what I was formerly loathe to believe.
>
> Critic: And with that admission all your fine theory about defence coefficients and what-not blows away in smoke!
>
> Author: Not a bit of it. For it is firmly founded on numerical fact.
>
> Critic: But you cannot say both that the war was caused by mutual interactions between populations and that a small clique planned it deliberately.
>
> Author: I think that those two statements are compatible, because leaders lead people where they are willing to be led.

Had Richardson lived to read the inside account of the Vietnam war (see The Pentagon Papers, 1971), his viewpoint would have been amply confirmed. In the next section we propose to show the compatibility of the two theories, that the onset of war is the automatic end product of an action-and-reaction "Richardson process," and that it is also the deliberate choice of national leaders.

THE ONSET OF WAR

"War is a continuation of State policy by other means." Research reported in this book not only supports this observation of von Clausewitz but indicates that the diplomacy-war sequence is a recurring phenomenon with a very regular period. The onset of international war, it appears, is predictably cyclic in nature with a two-phase cold war-hot war pattern.

Theoretical predictions that there might be a rhythm in the various national military budgets derive from Richardson's arms race equations. Since the two equations combine to form a single second order differential equation (see Appendix), possible solutions involve exponential growth and decay, and sinusoidal variation. Indeed, Murray Wolfson (1968) was able to show, by means of a pair of difference equations, that arms races could be highly unstable in a runaway fashion, or could reach a steady state which was either stable or oscillating with a long relaxation cycle.

If an arms race is characterized by two or more belligerent nations whose arms expenditures over time are more correlated with one another than with any other group of nations, then there have been three discernible arms races since 1945. The time period for the East-West arms race is 5.3 years, for the Middle East 2.7 years, and for the Far East the characteristic period is 6.8 years. Thirty-seven countries in all were found to correlate significantly with sine waves of the appropriate wave-length. Wars involving any of these 37 countries were listed by date of onset under the appropriate group (East-West, Middle East, Far East), multiple listings being included when more than one of the 37 countries was involved in any given war. These three lists of wars were also found to correlate significantly with the sine waves characterizing the three arms races. When the arms race data were lagged six months in time, the correlations were significantly higher; lists of larger wars were more highly correlated with the sine wave curves than were lists which included all wars.

Moyal found a five and 15 year periodicity in the onset of war from 1480 to 1900, while Denton and Singer found a 20-30 year periodicity in the amount of violence from 1820 to the present. They postulated a generation effect. From a list of interstate wars compiled by Singer, Small and Jones (1969), it can be ascertained that the duration of war varies with its intensity, from an average of less than one year for the smaller conflicts to about three years for the largest.

Singer and Small found that the more alliance commitments a nation makes, the more likely it is to be at war in the next several years, a fact which is consistent with the further finding that alliance partners tend to honour their commitments. Wallace discovered that alliances directly affect armed force levels, and that these increases lead to war, which lead him to conclude that increases in armed force levels (of 19th and 20th century nations) appeared to be the key factors in transforming the tensions generated by the structure of the international system into open belligerency.

When Rummel and Tanter examined the relationship between domestic strife—riots, revolutions and civil war—and foreign strife (including war), they found a significant positive correlation between the two when the domestic strife data were lagged by three years.

A content analysis of the public statements of former U. S. Secretary of State John Foster Dulles persuaded Holsti that, in Dulles' view, Soviet hostility and capability reached a maximum in 1954 and 1958, and a minimum in 1956.

These various strands of evidence are all consistent with the verbal statement of page 199 and with a causal two-phase theory of war. Territorial disagreements between neighbouring nations (or between groups within a nation) are reinforced by ideological differences. These ideological differences may be national, political, religious or class. Tension develops. The leaders become aggressive and escalate their arms; to increase their power still further they simultaneously form alliances with compatible allies. As the escalation proceeds, the leaders gain confidence, but under the strain of armaments, domestic conflict increases which slows down the military spending. Since both sides are engaged in this process, and since they interact with one another, the arms expenditures follow a natural sinusoidal rhythm as predicted by the Richardson arms race equations. The pendulum of armament increases starts to swing down. Though the rate of armament increases steadily diminishes, the arms level continues to grow (see Figure 7). At this point the military mind considers going to war for two reasons. One, the country is as strong as it will be for several years. And two, a war will tend to arrest the anticipated downward swing of military spending. Almost all wars therefore start just when the arms race is about to crank down, that is, they are out of phase with the rhythm of arms spending. The wars last an average of two years. When they are over, arms spending is increasing once more. Very occassionally a war will break out which is in phase with the arms spending cycle. When that happens (as it did in Korea under the influence of General Douglas MacArthur) military appropriations are positively reinforced and are therefore carried to unusually high levels. It is noteworthy that MacArthur took issue with Clausewitz' dictum; he believed that the military establishment should direct policy (Silvain, 1951.)

Dut to the regular impetus of war somewhere in an arms race system, the natural cycle of arms spending is maintained; moreover, under the stimulus of these shooting wars, the level of arms spending steadily increases. Finally, such an intolerable level of spending is reached that a massive war breaks out. Normal fluctuations in the arms race and the onset of medium-sized wars have a natural period of 5-6 years; while the onset of big wars has a natural period of 25-30 years. Why the arms race period should be five years is still in doubt. The 25-year cycle is likely a generation effect: a combination of older men in power (who fought in the last big war) now wanting to run a new one, and younger men (who never experienced war) now ready to fight. Richardson reports that from 1918 to about 1927 books about the 1914-18 war did not sell in England or in Germany; thereafter war novels revived with extreme intensity (1960b, p. 235.)

Implicit in the two-phase theory of war is thus a rather exact periodicity. Also implicit is the almost mechanical alteration between hot and cold war periods—while the arms race is escalating steadily war does not begin (see Figure 7), but when the rate falters, or soon after, one of the countries involved engages in international war since "war is a continuation of State policy by other means." The rhythm is shown in Figure 7 where the cyclic arms spending and the out-of-phase rate of increase of arms spending are shown for a hypothetical arms race.

A not unreasonable hypothesis might be that high levels and high rates of increase of armaments are more serious for nations caught up in an arms race, e.g. Sweden has a high level of arms, but is not involved in an arms race and has had no wars for over a century. To test the hypothesis, a revised threat index (see p. 153) was determined for the 51 countries for which military budgets are accurately known since 1948. The revised index gave additional weight to countries whose annual defence increments correlated with curves A, B, or C over the 20-year period (see Table 13) and therefore could be assumed to be part of one of the three arms races since 1945. The results were very satisfactory: four countries were predicted to be warlike and were still at peace by 1970

(Iran, Spain, Brazil and South Africa); two countries were predicted to be peaceful and were at war during the 1964-70 period (El Salvador and Honduras). The remaining 45 countries were correctly "predicted," so that just under 75 percent of the variance was accounted for by the revised threat index.

A composite plot of the sine wave curves describing the three arms races since 1945 shows peaks at 1945, 1950, 1956, 1958, 1961, 1964, 1967, 1972 and and 1979—the 1972 peak being the largest since 1945 (see Figure 8). According to the two-phase theory, alliances should occur in the major trough periods and therefore might have been expected in 1948-49 or 1954-55. In fact the OAS and NATO were formed in the first of these two periods while the Warsaw Pact and SEATO were formed in the second. Wars should have been expected in 1945-48, 1950-54, 1956-65, 1967-70; they should not have been expected in 1949, 1955, 1966, and 1971. All these "predictions" in fact came true.* There were 39 international wars or border conflicts during the 1946-71 period, according to the SIPRI Yearbook for 1968/69 and Facts and File. None of these wars began during the "forbidden" years (see Figure 8). There were also 23 wars where over 1,000 were killed which were either purely civil or else civil and international. None of these wars started during the forbidden years.* For smaller civil wars the arms race theory does not hold up so well, thus different indices must be sought. But for all international wars and the larger civil wars (over

* With the single exception of the Pakistan-India War in December, 1971 which started 6 months "too soon."

Figure 7

HOT WAR - COLD WAR PERIODICITY

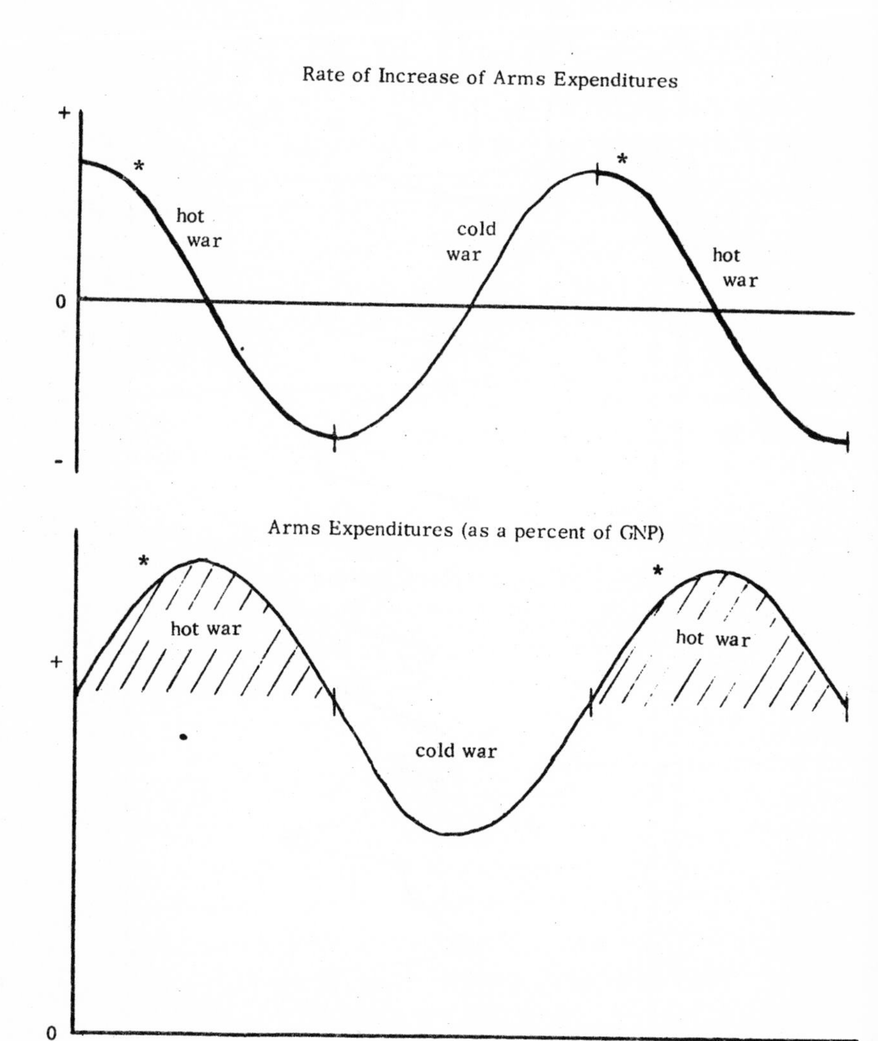

* Onset of biggest wars when rate of increase of arms expenditures and arms expenditures both large.

Figure 8

"PREDICTION" OF WAR

Composite plot of theoretical sine wave curves (rates of increase of arms expenditures) describing the three arms races since 1945 versus actual wars (all international wars plus the larger civil wars)

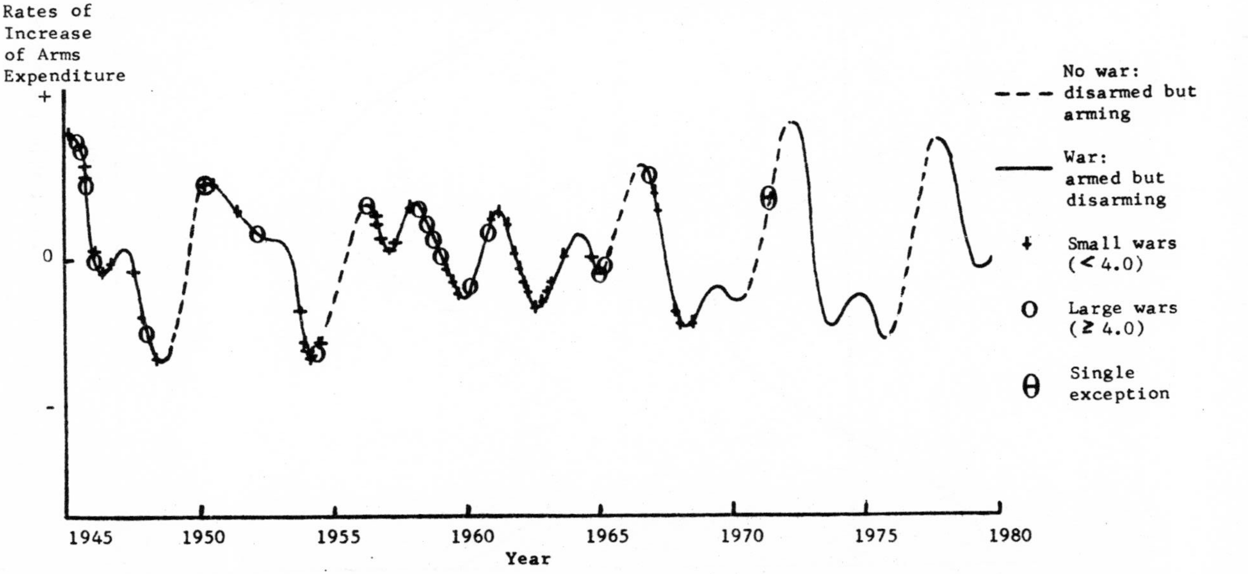

.1,000 killed) the theory accounts for 75 percent of the variance. Such predictive powers are remarkable.

The years from mid-1972 to the end of 1975 will be an extremely dangerous period (see Figure 8). It will require an almost superhuman forebearance on the part of political leaders if smaller wars are not to escalate into a conflagration. Were a number of substantial peace initiatives to be introduced instead of an escalation of war, the world could have renewed hope. Perhaps, for reasons yet unknown, there will be time. Perhaps, for reasons yet unknown, mankind will pass through this dark and foreboding period of history to a dazzling vision beyond. Even now, we may be standing on the threshold.

glossary

These are terms which may be found only in specialized scientific dictionaries, or which are so ambiguous as to require definition to explain how they are used in this book. Many of the definitions are from A Comprehensive Dictionary of Psychological and Psychoanalytical Terms by Horace B. English and Ava C. English.

aggression — the fighting instinct in animals or man which is directed against members of the same species.

altruism — desire to further the welfare of others.

anomy — the state of being without organization or system.

attitude — persistant mental state of readiness to react to a certain object or class of objects, not as they are conceived to be.

belief — an emotional acceptance of a proposition or doctrine based on what one considers adequate grounds.

correlation — the degree to which two or more variables vary together.

deviance — behaviours or attitudes not in accord with prevailing patterns or moral standards of a group.

ethology — study of animal behaviour in the natural habitat.

factor analysis — statistical method for determining the minimum number of factors required to explain the scores from a number of tests.

ideology — complex system of ideas, beliefs and attitudes that constitutes for an individual or group a total or extensive philosophy or world view.

imprinting – kind of learning characterized by occurrence in very early life, rapidity of acquisition, and relative insusceptibility to forgetting or extinction.

inhibiting mechanism – stimulus which automatically inhibits a certain restricted class of responses.

instinct – enduring tendency to act in an organized and biologically adaptive way that is characteristic of a given species.

institution – enduring organization of some aspect of collective life (social, political, economic, religious) controlled by rules, customs, rituals or laws.

ism – practice dominated by a theory.

love – desire to further the welfare of others and oneself.

multiple regression analysis – a method for computing the most probable value of one variable from the known values of several other variables.

opinion – acceptance of a proposition, supposedly nonemotional and based on factual evidence.

parameter – any constant in a mathematical equation of two or more variables.

releasing mechanism – stimulus which released automatically a certain restricted class of responses.

replicate – to repeat an experiment with all essentials unchanged.

variance – measure of the extent to which individual scores in a group differ from the mean of the group (the square of the standard deviation).

appendix

For convenience of manipulation, the Richardson arms race equations are generally expressed in the calculus form:

$$\frac{dx}{dt} = g + ky - ax \qquad (1)$$

$$\frac{dy}{dt} = h + lx - by \qquad (2)$$

where:

x and y represent the military expenditures of the two sides of a cold war;

g and h represent the grievance or ambition (contentment or goodwill) of each side, respectively;

k and l are the respective defence coefficients;

a and b are the respective fatigue coefficients;

$\frac{dx}{dt}$ and $\frac{dy}{dt}$ are the derivatives with respect to time of x and y.

Equations 1 and 2 are stable (i. e. x and y reach values which do not change over time) when kl is less than ab, unstable when kl is greater than ab. If g or h is positive, then y or x will be positive at the stable point; conversely, if g or h is negative, then y or x will be negative at the stable point (though a negative x or y is an undefined concept).

The addition of equations 1 and 2, if we let k = l and a = b, yields:

$$\frac{d(x + y)}{dt} = (g + h) + (k - a)(x + y) \qquad (3)$$

If $\frac{d(x+y)}{dt}$ and $x + y$ of equation 3 are plotted, the resulting straight line will intercept the y axis at $(g + h)$ and will have a slope of $(k - a)$.

The solution of equation 3 is:

$x + y = ce^{(k-a)t} - \frac{(g+h)}{(k-a)}$ where c is an arbitrary constant. (4)

The variables in equations 1 and 2 can be separated in the following way: differentiate equation 1 with respect to t, substitute equation 2 for $\frac{dy}{dt}$, substitute equation 1 for $\frac{dx}{dt}$ which yields:

$$(kh + bg) = \frac{d^2x}{dt^2} + (a + b)\frac{dx}{dt} + (ab - kl)x \qquad (5)$$

The solution of which is:

$$x = c_1 + c_2e^{At} + c_3e^{Bt} \qquad (6)$$

where $c_1 = \frac{kh + bg}{ab - kl}$, c_2 and c_3 are arbitrary constants
A and B are functions of a, b, k and l.

When: $4(ab - kl)$ is less than $(a + b)^2$ then x is a periodic function of time of the form:

$$x = c_1 + c_4e^{At}\cos(Bt + c_5) \qquad (7)$$

where c_4 and c_5 are arbitrary constants, A and B are functions of a, b, k and l.

Equation 4 says simply that the sum of the military expenditures of both sides of a cold war engaged in an arms race can remain constant (at c if $k = a$), can increase smoothly in exponential fashion (if k is greater than a) or can decrease smoothly in an exponential fashion (if k is less than a).

Equation 7 says simply that the expenditures of both sides can individually oscillate back and forth, though together they are increasing or decreasing in a smooth exponential fashion.

references

Abelson, Robert. A "Derivation" of Richardson's Equations. Journal of Conflict Resolution, 1963, 7, pp. 13-15.

Adorno, T.W., Frenkel-Brunswick, E., Levinson, D.J., and Sanford, R.N. The Authoritarian Personality. New York: Harper & Row, 1950.

Alcock, Norman Z. The Bridge of Reason. Oakville, Ontario: John Wilkes Press, 1961.

Alcock, Norman Z. An Empirical Measure of Internation Threat: Some Preliminary Implications for the Middle East Conflict. Papers of the Peace Research Society (International), 1970, 15.

Alcock, Norman Z. Prediction of International Violence. Peace Research, 1971, 3, 5.

Alcock, Norman Z., and Greenfield, Richard. Empirical Measure of Ideological Distance between Nations. Paper presented to Canadian Political Science Association Annual Meeting, University of Manitoba, Winnipeg, June 3, 1970.

Alcock, Norman Z., and Lowe, Keith. The Vietnam War as a Richardson Process. Journal of Peace Research, No. 2, pp. 105-112, 1969.

Alcock, Norman Z., Young, Christopher, and Kielly, Edward. Arms Race Regularities. Papers of the International Peace Research Association, 1971, 4.

Allee, W.C. The Social Life of Animals. Boston: Beacon Press, 1938.

Allport, Gordon W. The Nature of Prejudice. Reading, Mass.: Addison-Wesley Publishing Company, Inc., 1954.

Ardrey, Robert. African Genesis. New York: Dell Books, 1961.

Babst, D.V. A proposal on war research. Peace Research, 1970, 2, 1.

Benoit, Emile. Economic adjustments to disarmament. In: Disarmament and the Economy. New York: Harper & Row, 1963, pp. 271-300.

Benoit, Emile, and Boulding, Kenneth E. (eds.). Disarmament and the Economy. New York: Harper & Row, 1963.

Boulding, Kenneth E. Conflict and Defense: A General Theory. New York: Harper & Row, 1961.

Boulding, Kenneth E. Integrative aspects of the international system. In: Proceedings of the International Peace Research

Association. Assen: Van Gorcum, 1966.

Brody, Richard A. Some systematic effects of the spread of nuclear weapons technology: A study through simulation of a multi-nuclear future. Journal of Conflict Resolution, 1963, pp. 663-753.

Cajori, Florian. A History of Physics. New York: Macmillan, 1929.

Carthy, J.D., and Ebling, F.J. (eds.). The Natural History of Aggression. London: Academic Press Inc., 1964.

Comrey, A. L., and Newmeyer, J. A. Measurement of radical-conservatism. Journal of Social Psychology, 1965, 67, pp. 357-369.

Coon, Carleton S. Origin of Races. New York: Alfred A. Knopf, 1965.

Dahlstrom, W. G., and Welsh, G. S. An MMPI Handbook. Minneapolis: University of Minnesota Press, 1960.

Denton, Frank. Some Regularities in International Conflict, 1920-1949. Background, 1966, 9, 4, pp. 283-96.

Druckman, Daniel. Ethnocentrism in the Inter-Nation simulation. Journal of Conflict Resolution, 1968, 12, pp. 45-68.

Easton, David, and Hess, Robert D. The child's political world. Midwest Journal of Political Science, 1962, 6, 3, pp. 229-246.

Easton, David, and Dennis, Jack. The child's image of government. American Academy of Political and Social Science, 1965, 361, pp. 40-57.

Eckhardt, William. Ideology and personality in social attitudes. Peace Research Reviews, 1969a, 3 (2), whole issue.

Eckhardt, William. Factors of Militarism. Journal of Peace Research, 1969b, 6 (2), pp. 123-132.

Eckhardt, William. Cross-cultural Conservatism. Peace Research, 1970a, 2 (5), p. 7.

Eckhardt, William. Cross-cultural Militarism. Peace Research, 1970b, 2 (6), p. 9.

Eckhardt, William. Cross-cultural Religiosity. Peace Research, 1970c, 2 (9), pp. 19-20.

Eckhardt, William. Cross-cultural Attitudes toward World Government. Peace Research, 1971, 3 (12), p. 14.

Eckhardt, William, and Alcock, Norman Z. Ideology and personality in war/peace attitudes. The Journal of Social Psychology, 1970, 81, pp. 105-116.

Eckhardt, William, and Lentz, Theodore F. Factors of War/Peace Attitudes. Peace Research Reviews, 1967, 1 (5).

Eckhardt, William, Manning, Morris, Morgan, Carl, Subotnik, Leo, and Tinker, Lorena-Jeanne. Militarism in our culture today. Journal of Human Relations, 1967, 15 (4), pp. 532-537.

Economic Intelligence Unit. The Economic Effects of Disarmament. London: United World Trust, 1963.

Education Advisory Committee of the Parliamentary Group for World Government, London, 1965.

Ehrlich, Paul R., and Anne H. Population, Resources, Environment. San Francisco: W.H. Freeman and Co., 1970.

Eibl-Eibesfeldt, Irenoius. Ethology: The Biology of Behavior. New York: Holt Rinehart and Winston, 1970.

Einstein, Albert, and Infeld, Leopold. The Evolution of Physics. New York: Simon and Schuster, Inc., 1938.

English, Horace B., and English, Ava C. A Comprehensive Dictionary of Psychological and Psychoanalytical Terms. New York: Longmans, Green and Co., Inc., 1958.

Eysenck, H.J. Manual of the Mandsley Personality Inventory. London: University of London Press, 1959.

Finlay, D., Iversen, C., and Raser, J. Handbook for Multi-National Student Survey. La Jolla, California: Western Behavioral Science Institute, 1969.

Freud, Sigmund. Reflecting on war and death (1915). In: Great Books of the Western World, Vol. 54. Chicago: Encyclopedia Britannica Inc., 1952.

Freud, Sigmund. Why War? (1932). Collected Papers, 5. New York: Basic Books, 1959.

Fromm, Erich. The Art of Loving. Montreal: Bantam Books, Inc., 1956.

Genovés, Santiago. Is Peace Inevitable? New York: Walker and Company, 1970.

Goldschmidt, Walter. Man's Way. Cleveland: The World Publishing Co., 1959.

Guetzkow, Harold, and Jensen, Lloyd. Research activities on simulated international processes. Background, 1966, 9 (4), pp. 261-274.

Haas, Michael. Societal approaches to the study of war. Journal of Peace Research, 1965, 2 (4), pp. 306-323.

Haddow, Alexander. In: Penrose, Margaret (ed.). Pathogenesis of War. London: H. K. Lewis and Co., 1963.

Holsti, Ole R. The belief system and national images: A case study. Journal of Conflict Resolution, 1962, 6, pp. 244-52.

Laulicht, Jerome. An analysis of Canadian foreign policy attitudes. In: Peace Research Society: Papers, III, 1965a, pp. 121-136.

Laulicht, Jerome. Canadian foreign policy attitudes: Some major conclusions. International Social Science Journal, 1965b, 17, pp. 472-486.

Laulicht, Jerome. Public opinion and foreign policy decisions. Journal of Peace Research, 1965c, 2(1), pp. 147-169.

Laulicht, Jerome, and Alcock, N. Z. The Support of Peace Research. Journal of Conflict Resolution, 1966, 10, pp. 198-208.

Laulicht, Jerome, and Martin, John. The Vietnam War Game. New Society, January 27, 1966.

Laulicht, Jerome, and Strong, George. In Your Opinion. Vol. II. Clarkson, Ontario: Canadian Peace Research Institute, 1967.

Lenin, V. I. Socialism and War. (2nd ed.) Moscow: Foreign Language Publishing House, 1915.

Lilly, John C. Man and Dolphin. New York: Doubleday and Co., Inc., 1961.

Lorenz, Konrad Z. King Solomon's Ring. London: Methuen & Co., Ltd., 1952.

Lorenz, Konrad Z. On Aggression. New York: Harcourt, Brace & World, Inc., 1966.

McNeil, Elton B. Violence and human development. Annals of the American Academy of Political and Social Science, 1966, 364.

Meerloo, Joost A. M. That Difficult Peace. New York: Channel Press, 1961.

Mills, C. Wright. The Causes of World War III. New York: Simon & Schuster, Inc., 1958.

Montagu, Ashley. The Cultured Man. Cleveland, Ohio: The World Publishing Co., 1958.

Mowat, Farley. Never Cry Wolf. New York: Dell Books, 1963.

Moyal, J. G. Distribution of Wars in Time. Journal of the Royal Statistical Society, 1949, 112, pp. 446-58.

Myrdal, Gunnar. Challenge to Affluence. London: Victor Gollancz, Ltd., 1963.

Naroll, Raoul. Does military deterrence deter? Trans-Action, 1966, 3 (2), 14-20.

Newcombe, Alan. Development of an Inter-nation Tensiometer. Papers of the Peace Research Society (International), August 1969.

Newcombe, Hanna, Ross, Michael, and Newcombe, Alan. United Nations Voting Patterns. International Organization, 1970, 24 (1), pp. 100-121.

Noel-Baker, Philip. The Private Manufacture of Armaments, London: John Calder, 1937.

Noel-Baker, Philip. The Arms Race. London: John Calder, 1958.

Osgood, Charles E. An Alternative to War or Surrender. Urbana, Illinois: University of Illinois Press, 1962.

Patel, Surendra J. Economic consequences of disarmament. Bulletin of Atomic Scientists, 1962, 18 (11).

Paul, John, and Laulicht, Jerome. In Your Opinion: Leaders' and Voters' Attitudes on Defence and Disarmament. Clarkson, Ontario: Canadian Peace Research Institute, 1963.

Peace Research Abstracts. Oakville, Ontario: Canadian Peace Research Institute.

Pentagon Papers. New York: New York Times, 1971.

Pylyshyn Z. Private communications, 1966.

Radlow, Robert. An experimental study of cooperation in the Prisoner's Dilemma Game. Journal of Conflict Resolution, 1965, 9, pp. 221-27.

Rapoport, Anatol. Fights, Games, and Debates. Ann Arbor, Michigan: University of Michigan Press, 1960.

Rapoport, Anatol. Games which simulate deterrence and disarmament. Peace Research Review, 1967, 1 (4), pp. 1-76.

Raser, John R., and Crow, Wayman J. A simulation study of deterrence theories. In: Proceedings of the International Peace Research Association. Assen: Van Gorcum, 1966, pp. 146-165.

Reves, Emery. Anatomy of Peace. New York: Harper & Row, Publishers, 1945.

Richardson, Lewis F. Statistics of Deadly Quarrels. Pittsburgh: Boxwood Press, 1960a.

Richardson, Lewis F. Arms and Insecurity. Pittsburgh: Boxwood Press, 1960b.

Rokeach, Milton. The Open and Closed Mind: Investigations into the Nature of Belief Systems and Personality Systems. New York: Basic Books, 1960.

Rosenbluth, Gideon. Planning for Peace – The Economics of Disarmament in Canada. Toronto: Macmillan, 1967.

Rummel, R.J. Dimensions of conflict behavior within nations, 1946-59. Journal of Conflict Resolution, 1966, 10, pp. 65-73.

Russell, Bertrand. Human Society in Ethics and Politics, New York: Mentor, 1952.

Russell, Elbert W. Christianity and Militarism. Peace Research Reviews, 1971, 4 (3), whole issue.

Russett, B.M., Alker, H.R., Deutsch, K.W., Lasswell, H.D. World Handbook of Political and Social Indicators. New Haven, Connecticut: Yale University Press, 1964.

Silvain, Rene. Clausewitz et la guerre de Coree. Revue Politique et Parlementaire, 611, 1951.

Singer, J. David, Small, Melvin, and Jones, Susan. The Wages of War: a Statistical Handbook, 1816-1965. Ann Arbor: University of Michigan, 1969.

Singer, J. David, and Small, Melvin. National Alliance Commitments and War Involvement, 1815-1945. Papers of the Peace Research Society (International), 1965, 5, pp. 109-140.

SIPRI Yearbook of World Armaments and Disarmament 1968/69. Stockholm: Almgvist and Wiksele, 1970.

Smoker, Paul. Fear in the arms race: A mathematical study. Journal of Peace Research, 1964, 1 (1), pp. 55-64.

Smoker, Paul. Trade, defense, and the Richardson theory of arms races: A seven nation study. Journal of Peace Research, 1965, 2 (2), pp. 161-176.

Smoker, Paul. The arms race: A wave model. Peace Research Society (International) Papers, 1966, IV, pp. 41-62.

Tanter, Raymond. Dimensions of conflict behavior within and between nations, 1958-60. Journal of Conflict Resolution, 1966, 10, pp. 41-64.

Terhune, Kenneth W. National aspiration, loyalty, and internationalism. Journal of Peace Research, 1965, 2 (3), pp. 277-287.

Terhune, Kenneth W. Personality Factors in Experimental Studies of International Conflict. Paper at Conference of CPREA, Sherbrooke, Quebec, June 11-12, 1966.

Triandis, Harry C., and Davis, Earl E. Race and Belief as determinants of behavioral intentions. Journal of Personality and Social Psychology, 1965, 2 (5), pp. 715-725.

U.S. Arms Control and Disarmament Agency. The economic and social consequences of disarmament. ACDA Publication, 1962, 6, July.

Voevodsky, John. Quantitative Behavior of Warring Nations. Journal of Psychology, 1969, 72, pp. 269-292.

Wallace, Michael D. The Onset of International War, 1820-45: A Preliminary Model. University of British Columbia, 1970, (mimeo).

Wolfson, Murray. A Mathematical Model of the Cold War. Papers of the Peace Research Society (International), 1968, 9.

Wright, Quincy. A Study of War. Chicago: University of Chicago Press, 1942.

Zinnes, Dina A. Hostility in international decision-making. Journal of Conflict Resolution, 1962, 6 (3), pp. 236-243.

index

Race, 15, 196